OUR CALLING TO FULFILL

OUR CALLING TO FULFILL

Wesleyan Views of the Church in Mission

Edited by
M. Douglas Meeks

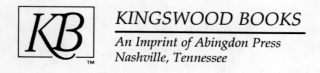

KINGSWOOD BOOKS
An Imprint of Abingdon Press
Nashville, Tennessee

OUR CALLING TO FULFILL
WESLEYAN VIEWS OF THE CHURCH IN MISSION

Library of Congress Cataloging-in-Publication Data

Oxford Institute of Methodist Theological Studies (12th : 2007)
  Our calling to fulfill : Wesleyan views of the church in mission / edited by M. Douglas Meeks.
     p. cm.
  Essays from the Twelfth Oxford Institute of Methodist Theological Studies, Aug. 2007.
  Includes bibliographical references.
  ISBN 978-1-426-70049-1 (pbk. : alk. paper)
  1. Mission of the church. 2. Methodist Church—Doctrines. I. Meeks, M. Douglas.
II. Title.
  BV601.8.O94 2007
  262'.07—dc22

                                                                            2009020873

09 10 11 12 13 14 15 16 17 18—10 9 8 7 6 5 4 3 2 1
MANUFACTURED IN THE UNITED STATES OF AMERICA

To Nora Quiroga Boots, with gratitude for her leadership
in Methodist mission

CONTENTS

ACKNOWLEDGMENTS

I would like to express my gratitude for the excellent editorial work of Blair Gilmer Meeks and for editing suggestions made by Carolyn Davis and Sarah Sanderson-Doughty.

M. Douglas Meeks

CHAPTER ONE

A HOME FOR THE HOMELESS: VOCATION, MISSION, AND CHURCH IN WESLEYAN PERSPECTIVE

M. Douglas Meeks

The twelfth Oxford Institute of Methodist Theological Studies, meeting at Christ Church, the Oxford college of John and Charles Wesley, took as its theme "To Serve the Present Age, My Calling to Fulfill." In the tercentenary year of his birth it was obviously appropriate to take this famous line from a hymn of Charles Wesley's as the Institute's theme. How to serve the present age with anything approximating a Christian calling, however, is a matter of considerable complication. Seven Methodist theologians from Africa, Latin America, Asia, Europe, and North America assumed the challenge in presentations from which the essays comprised in this book stemmed.

The challenge of addressing the theme of "vocation, mission, and church" in our time is immense. Where can Christian calling take place and be nurtured in our highly secularized societies? Has not mission, at least as practiced by Christians in the developed societies, been utterly discredited, charged with being complicit in spreading globally the political economies and cultures of competitive markets? Didn't the ecumenical movement seemingly collapse because of antagonism from various parts of the world church about the meaning and practice of mission? Do we not hear a cry from Christians on every continent about an "ecclesiological deficit"? And what, after all, does the variegated Wesleyan tradition have to offer in addressing these questions?

It is not surprising that some tensions and different perspectives appear in these essays, since these questions are addressed from the perspective of different continents and from churches in different cultural, political, and economic situations. The three essayists from Africa, Asia, and Latin America make us keenly aware that Methodism was delivered to their regions by missionaries who had adapted Methodism to the nineteenth-century North American and European contexts. In the process some of the most important theological contributions of Wesley were lost. Even when the themes are the same, contemporary Methodism in Africa, Asia, and Latin America develops differing views of discipleship, sanctification, and church from Methodism in the developed countries. Discipleship in mainland China during the Cultural Revolution or in South Africa under apartheid looks different from its developed world expressions. But precisely because the essays offer different slants on these urgent matters, they also offer a Wesleyan conferring that is resourceful and encouraging for world Methodism.

All the essays fall within the creative tension of two questions: How can the church simultaneously serve Christ and the world if it lives according to the standards of the world and does not stand apart from the world? But, on the other hand, how can the church serve Christ and the world if it does not stand in solidarity with the world God loves with God's whole being? The essays wager that there is a distinctive Wesleyan answer to the church's ancient question: How to be in the world but not of it? The Wesleyan response has to do with holding together in tension inward and outward holiness, worship and mission in the world, grace given and grace lived, and preparatory waiting and prophetic act.

Several themes emerge as these Wesleyan theologians wrestle with how to account for (1) the connection between the doctrine of the church and God's own life and work, (2) the human constituency of the church, (3) the church's mission in a time of global crisis, (4) Christian vocation, (5) the Wesleyan centrality of sanctification, and (6) human dignity in a pluralist world.

THE CHURCH AS GOD'S CREATION

William Willimon maintains that for Methodists the burning question of "ecclesiological deficit" is at heart a failure to understand Wesley's insistence that the church is an expression of the life and work of God. We try to craft "church" before we ask, *Who is God, and what is God doing?* The starting point for a doctrine of the church should rather be the worship of the God whose "processions" of Father, Son, and Holy Spirit show forth God's self-giving to God's creation. The inward and outer movements of God's triune life vivify the rhythm of the church's inner and outer life.

Willimon decries the subjectivity of some Wesleyan theology that tries to derive the church from human affectivity and will. This descent into subjectivity serves an accommodation to consumerism and promotes an unsure activism in the church that does not follow where God proceeds. The proclamation of the church is reduced to getting with the "message" rather than transforming life through an encounter in Jesus with the triune God. "Because of our limp theology, our anthropology becomes too stable, and the purpose of our preaching is adjustment, confirmation rather than conversion. Preaching thus becomes another means of self-cultivation as well as a well-reasoned defense against true transformation." A Wesleyan ecclesiology will stress that our vocation and service "to the present age" are a call for transformative justice that begins with our own transformation by God's grace. We dare not think of outward mission without our inward conversion.

But it is Wesley's "lively trinitarian God of constant processions" that also leads to Wesley's emphasis on God's presence among the suffering and the excluded. It is not our subjectivity that makes the true church present. Rather, the church is present where Christ is present. According to 1 Peter, Christ is present among the *paraoikoi*, the strangers, the homeless who dwell beyond the hearth. The church as Christ's "home for the homeless," then, must go beyond itself to find itself in Christ. Any Wesleyan view of a calling into the church and into the church's mission to the world will focus on the power God gives us for intimacy with the poor. There is in Methodism a widespread sense that the coming church will look different from the present church, though we struggle to imagine what will emerge. What we do know from a Wesleyan identity is that we will meet the future of the church in God's presence with the poor.

THE CHURCH AS THE WHOLE PEOPLE OF GOD

All the authors in this volume deal in one way or another with how God constitutes the church as a crucial issue in constructing an ecclesiology. Lung-kwong Lo develops his ecclesiology through a series of images of the church as "the people of God" and relates these images to the Asian concept of *minjung*, a term meaning "the mass of the people." Transcending the boundaries of social classes, *minjung* represents people who suffer different kinds of oppression. In a similar fashion, but from the context of South Africa, Ivan Abrahams calls on the African concepts of *Ubuntu* and *Botho* (meaning "a person is a person because of other persons") as a way of speaking about the humaneness and dignity of the diverse people Christ seeks to bring into the economy of life. In the Latin American context Paulo Mattos points to the early Wesleyan revival's focus on the poor as the recipients of the gospel's promise as a needed direction for the Brazilian Methodist Church. In fact, all three authors stress that the Methodist movement was started as a reform movement inside the Church of England and was directed toward the poor.

One value of remembering early Methodism as a movement to the poor is its reflection of the New Testament depiction of the church as "home for the homeless." As a way of discussing the difficulty of thinking and living the church in Latin America, Mattos traces some of the weaknesses of North American Methodism brought to Brazil by missionaries. Wesley's understanding of the corporate nature of Christianity, expressed in bands, classes, societies, and conferences, was subordinated to North American middle-class individualism and salvation as a private matter. He discusses, among other factors, the effect of the camp meeting's emotional impact on lessening the corporate nature of conference, upsetting the balance between social and personal holiness.

The view of the church that Lo, Abrahams, and Mattos are developing is of a "congregation in the wilderness," on the move, not defined by the confining stasis of its surroundings, a community always under construction by the power of the Holy Spirit, held together by the risen Christ's self-giving to the lost and forsaken.

THE CHURCH SHAPED BY MISSION

After five decades of severe crisis in relating Christian mission and the *oikoumene*, there is no doubt that we must have a rebirth of both and that neither can be reborn without the other. The ecumenical movement in the last century was epitomized by the conviction that the being of the church is the *missio Dei*, that is, the triune God's way of redeeming the world. It was often said that the church *is* mission. But churches in the developed and developing worlds disagreed on the meaning and method of mission. In the developing world the church is usually a minority institution, often a movement of oppressed people, whereas in some countries of the West it has been a majority, sanctioned if not misused by the powerful. The beginnings of the Wesleyan movement are more reflected by the former. What in the Wesleyan tradition could contribute today to new perceptions and practices of mission?

The authors of this volume generally agree that regaining a sense of being a Wesleyan *movement* would be salutary to Methodist churches. This is, of course, easier said than done. Methodist churches in different parts of the world relate to the power structures in their contexts in different ways. With the present enormous crisis of the global fiscal system, all parts of the world may be faced with a radical redefinition of power. What until only recently was seen as the imperial power of the United States and Europe suddenly looks quite different. We are entering a period of great danger, especially if countries losing economic control resort to military means of maintaining their superiority, but it may also be a time when power can be reimagined and more justly distributed in the world.

If churches that for more than a century have shaped themselves according to corporate economy can reshape themselves to stand in greater solidarity with those who are excluded from the reigning political economy, they could create new models of mission as cooperative seeking of human dignity for all and equity in the goods necessary for the flourishing of human life.

A concern that looms large in this volume's treatment of mission is slavery. Both Abrahams and Mattos draw heavily on John Wesley's stand on abolition of slavery to formulate a calling for Wesleyan churches to join the struggle to end today's slavery brought on by globalized capitalism. Even chattel slavery, the enormous worldwide traffic in human beings, has not ended in our time, and there are many other kinds of slavery, including a plethora of addictions in our consumerist societies. Here again we must be cognizant of Wesley's insistence on the inner and outer freedom from slavery. Paul spoke of our ultimate captivity being our "slavery to the law of sin and death." A new understanding of mission in the oikoumene in our time will emphasize this universal threat of slavery in the heart of every human being and every culture. The grace that works through love in a mission serving God's justice in the world has to work also in freeing us from our spiritual captivity to falsely constructed systems of security.

CHRISTIAN VOCATION

Who will receive a vocation to enter into this mission? In what place and time in our self-absorbed cultures can a person hear and respond to such a call? Are people hearing the calling of God to mission in Methodist and Wesleyan congregations throughout the world? Baptism is a participation in God's love that is at once a call to mission, a call to give oneself to God's mission of redeeming the world. But through baptism the Holy Spirit calls the ministry of the church into being because there can be no mission without the community of disciples who follow Jesus. The call to mission entails and necessitates the call to church. In Christ the vocation is universal, but the call to mission comes to persons and communities in particular times and places. To the "gospel feast" all for whom Christ has died are called, but the feast is held as an occasion within the turmoil, suffering, and joy of a definite place. The limitless nature of God's grace comes to rest in a setting that is just as peculiar as the everyday relations of a community.

Tim Macquiban claims that Methodists can learn much about the universal and particular character of Christian calling from Charles Wesley's hymns. In the same way Wesley in his "re-creative thought enabled Scripture to speak to our human condition in what it means to be a Christian, we can re-create a Wesleyan understanding of our calling, vocation, and work in the twenty-first century to serve the present age." Wesley's hymns join biblical narrative with grace-filled experience to help shape our Methodist identity and give us a deeper understanding of our calling. The vocational hymns then become "for us subversive acts of profound hope in a fractured world making sense of who we are and how we act in this Wesleyan tradition, connecting heart and mind, worship and work."

Several aspects of Christian vocation are prominent in Wesley's hymns. A constant theme in the hymns is: no vocation without following Jesus. A Wesleyan sense of vocation to service and mission is centered in the tradition of the *imitatio Christi*. Because vocations are decided by the diverse gifts given to members of the congregation, discerning the gifts of baptized persons is a primary task of the congregation. Making fruitful the gifts given one is a primary responsibility of a person called and sent into Christ's ministry of healing and reconciliation. God gives gifts for ministry that are appropriate to an individual person and to the time and place in which the person is called.

A Wesleyan emphasis is that vocation takes place in and through the experience of living the gospel. Calling means actually living the gifts God gives through the gospel: repentance, giving, forgiving, and hospitality. Vocation is the wrenching experience of giving up one's take on the world and being grasped by God's love of the world. It is giving one's life in response to God's giving Godself for the redemption of the world (John 3:16). It is forgiving those who sin against me as God has forgiven me. It is, as Charles so often reminds us, extending hospitality to the stranger, making home for the homeless.

For Methodists to serve the present age in renewed mission and oikoumene would mean a revived practice of vocation in congregation and families. The original Wesleyan insistence that the ministry of clergy exists for the sake of the formation of the ministry of the laity is decisive to vocation in our time.

It is also imperative for us to regain the Wesleyan sense of the way service opens up the experience of grace. The vocation of "making room for the stranger" is already an experience of the joy of the kingdom. As Macquiban makes clear, Charles Wesley's hymns have a vivid sense of the way the Holy Spirit brings the promised future into present work and suffering so that heaven is already experienced under the conditions of history.

HOLINESS AND LOVE

As Marjorie Suchocki, Lo, and Macquiban amply demonstrate, sanctification is the substance of Wesleyan ecclesiology. According to Suchocki, "our self-understanding as Methodists and our contribution to ecumenical ecclesiology are to clarify the sense in which Christian perfection illumines the traditional formulations of the church." Sanctification is the "process of being continuously formed in the image of God." Sanctification is participation in God's love and therefore love of neighbor. According to 1 Corinthians 1, the power of God is God's self-giving in the cross of Christ. Love is the power by which God creates, provisions, and redeems the creation. If love is the power of God's self-giving that gives us the power to serve life, it is not too strong to say that sanctification is the milieu of vocation, the substance of the church, and the power of mission.

The church is not *sui generis*, as many schemes for trying to revive the church in our time seem to think. As Suchocki expresses the point, "The church exists to participate in the love of God, and if God loves the world, and if love cares for the fullness of well-being, then the church, which is strengthened in love through word and sacrament, necessarily expends itself in service to the needs of the world." Sanctification cannot be undertaken singly but only in the company of disciples. This is so because love adapts to the condition of the loved one and thus constantly occasions the transformation of each that brings into being the community of all. Precisely because perfection is empowerment for love, its sign is the "webs of care for one another's well-being."

Christian perfection cannot be separated from the reality of word and sacrament that serve the making present and incarnating of God's love. Word and sacrament are God's means of grace by which we are formed in the image of God. They shape our lives in the here and now according to the love that has been expressed in Jesus and for the sake of what is coming in God's grace.

Sanctification as God's gift that brings us into the communion of God's love is the presupposition of our service of the present age.

THE CHURCH IN A PLURALIST SOCIETY: THE GOSPEL AND HUMAN DIGNITY

But how practically are we to serve the present age? There may be a dawning realization that unless the world community creates a more just economy and a wiser care of the earth, the present age is in dire jeopardy. But how should the ecumenical church work cooperatively in serving this broken world? Robin Lovin's essay makes a crucial contribution here in seeking a way to establish human rights that could be understood by churches in different political and economic contexts as an essential component of mission. Lovin is quite aware of the suspicion of human rights on many fronts, and he takes seriously the modern conflict between vocation as delimitation of work roles and the modern Enlightenment ideal of human dignity.

The Wesleyan movement, argues Lovin, is a creative resource for contemporary humanizing mission because it occurred in the transition to modernity and yet was able to affirm the value of both work and human dignity. Perhaps no theologian esteemed work within one's vocation more than did John Wesley. But at the same time, Wesley recognized the God-given dignity of the poor and others who could not gain social recognition by work. It is this simple dignity that Wesley believed fitted the poor and marginalized for a Christian vocation. Following Jesus, Wesley insisted that redemption of the poor, no matter how poor, included their work in service to others. On the other hand, Wesley taught that those who thought their dignity precluded their need to work are deeply mistaken. The gospel's gift of dignity, purely and simply, entails vocation and work.

Lovin argues that serving the present age in mission will mean that Christian mission cannot be closed in on itself. In Wesley and the early Methodists we find a pluralistic understanding of politics and society. Pluralism exists because "human goods exist in the forms that people create and maintain in concrete social situations, in their interactions with one another across all the lines of race, religion, ethnicity, and class that initially divide them." These goods can be understood theologically and legally in various ways, but no institution, including church and state, can claim to be the source of their existence or the definer of their meaning for those who share in them. The God-given dignity of human beings means that they cannot be sacrificed to the workings of markets, movements, ideologies, or laws. Only when states and international institutions recognize the reality of the conditions of human dignity will we be able to make declarations of human rights actually effective. Thus, Lovin proposes, to serve the present age and fulfill our calling, our mission should be focused on creating the conditions under which all human beings can experience what human dignity means.

Lovin is proposing something like a Wesleyan "experimental" mission. He urges that "marginal Christianity" is effective when it depends on shared experience rather than expecting its marching orders from above. Like Wesley, it should go ahead with what should and can be done, and ask for forgiveness later. It should depend less on its own programs and rather support people in accomplishing what they are seeking, and thereby transform the "order of social possibilities." Accepting and fulfilling this calling, says Lovin, "will not just be a service to our neighbors, but a working out of our own salvation. It will not be just an application of the gospel of Jesus Christ to a separate, secular reality, but a way of understanding how the love of God fills all things and reaches every person."

All of these essays attest to God's abundant grace and yet do so with eyes open to the contradictions of God's grace in Methodist churches as well as in the world. In the midst of continuing warfare, fragile governments, massive hunger, and threatened world depression, we live with a chastened hope. Our calling is to work together with all humanity to shape the different future God promises and thereby serve the present age. By serving God's promise of home for the homeless, we anticipate that time when God will make this world God's home.

CHAPTER TWO

What If Wesley Was Right?

William H. Willimon

What if Wesley was right?[1]

Silly question. We attend to Wesley because we all believe that Wesley was right, not right about everything, to be sure ("beware of panegyric, particularly in London"),[2] but right about the things that matter. And if Wesley was right, about what he was most right about, then perhaps we should be uncomfortable. I suspect that some of us attend to Wesley not so much because we believe Wesley was right, but because we think he was interesting. We have a Wesleyan affinity, we are part of the "Wesleyan tradition," we are curious about Wesley, or we find him useful in explaining something else that interests us more than Wesley: "Wesley, the organizational genius of the eighteenth century," or "Wesley, the Tory for all seasons," or some other merely academic interest. As a sometime academic myself, I have some admiration for those who can muster enthusiasm for such matters. But not much.

What if "our Old Daddy" (Asbury's somewhat mocking title for Wesley) was not just interesting but also *right*? We may be uncomfortable because if Wesley was right in what he thought and taught, then we may be wrong. To ask, *What if Wesley was right?* is to allow ourselves to be challenged by Wesley's grasp of reality.

And if we should be so engaged by him, interrogated by him, and if we find ourselves thinking about God with him, why, we might again become theologians. We might again believe that there is nothing more important to talk about and no one more important to listen to than God.

So if you have a mainly archaeological interest in Wesley as a set of ancient texts, a man who was remarkable rather than a man who was right, this essay may have nothing to say to you.

If Wesley was right, then a conference about Wesley can be dangerous as we endeavor to protect ourselves against Wesley by talking about him rather than daring to allow him to talk to us. (Wesley's dreaded "almost Christian"[3] comes in many forms.)

To answer *What if Wesley was right?* we need to think what Wesley thought. The most challenging task of thinking with Wesley is that we must become theologians. That is, we must begin where he began.[4] To read Wesley is to be in the presence of a man who has been assaulted by the living, speaking, active, interactive personality of the triune God. To read Wesley's *Journals* is to be with a man who is driven, moment by moment (even the most mundane), thought by thought (even the most trivial) by a robust, resourceful God. (Only a man who had the stupidest idea of luck—which Wesley did not—or the most extravagant notions of particular providence—which Wesley did—could rely upon casting lots as a method of intellectual discernment.)[5]

WHAT IF WESLEY WAS RIGHT ABOUT GOD?

Wesley was more a medieval theologian than he was a modern one. He inherited the robust trinitarian faith that had been worked out in the early centuries of the church. God is not an idea, an abstraction, a source of meaning, a wholly other, a general concept, or a technique to help us make it through the day; God is the One who presently, directly speaks, creates, intrudes, demands, commands, passionately loves, continually transforms. Wesley's biblical interpretation is a sort of anti-interpretation in which he assumes that God speaks through Scripture, every word of it. Rather than assume that the task of the interpreter is to make the text more meaningful to sophisticated, modern people who drive Volvos, Wesley seems to assume that the task of the text is to make the interpreters' lives more difficult.

As Wesley wrote to his father, at the heart of the Methodist movement is a "habitual lively sense of our being only instruments in His hand, who can do all things either with or without any instrument."[6] Much of American popular religion is instrumental—religion valued on the basis of its alleged personal or social utility. Wesley assumes that the reader is instrumental to the biblical text.

What respectful, deferential, intellectually constrained Deist could write so sensuously?

1   Rise my soul with ardor rise,
            Breathe thy wishes to the skies;
            Freely pour out all thy mind,
            Seek, and thou art sure to find;
            Ready art thou to receive?
            Readier is thy God to give.

3   Friend of sinners, King of saints,
            Answer my minutest wants,
            All my largest thoughts require,
            Grant me all my heart's desire,
            Give me, till my cup run o'er,
            All, and infinitely more.[7]

Wesley assumes a God of plenitude, a God who is extravagantly, abundantly revelatory ("my cup run o'er, / All, and infinitely more"). Most of us have been trained, when we're thinking about God, to assume deprivation. We lack enough information about God to speak with any authority about God.

6   Since the Son hath made me free,
            Let me taste my liberty,
            Thee behold with open face,
            Triumph in thy saving grace,
            Thy great will delight to prove,
            Glory in thy perfect love.

7   Since the Son hath bought my peace,
          Mine thou art, as I am his:[8]
          Mine the Comforter I see,
          Christ is full of grace for me:
          Mine (the purchase of his blood)
          All the plenitude of God.

If Wesley was right about God, then we are wrong. We hear Wesley from within a dysfunctional family where death is normal, and we have become so respectful of God that we have silenced God. John Milbank accuses contemporary theology of dying under the grip of a "false modesty" in which theology finds it impossible to declare anything with conviction. We say that we are so respectful of the ineffable mystery of God. In reality, we are reluctant to speak about God for fear that in the process we might discover a God who says something definitive and authoritative to us. Spent Calvinism, sliding into a renovated Deism, has triumphed. God is all distant concept, abstraction, and essence, a never-speaking, revealing, troubling subject. We've got just enough God to give our lives a kind of spiritual tint without so much God as to interfere with our running the world as we please.

I have just listened to the taped sermons of sixty of the preachers who are under my care. Many of their sermons were lively and engaging, and most congregations would hear them gladly on a Sunday. Yet in a depressing majority of these sermons there was little indication that the content of the sermon or the engine driving the proclamation was the gospel of Jesus Christ. Other than that, they were fine sermons.

One sermon began well enough, the Second Sunday of Christmas, Luke 2, young Jesus putting the temple elders through their paces, abandoning Mom and Dad. After reading the text, and noting Jesus' amazing ability to stupefy professional scholars, the preacher then sailed off into a veritable shopping list of things *we* needed to do. We were told that we must resolve, in the coming year, to be more proficient in study of God's word. We should strive to "increase in wisdom and in stature." We ought to spend more time with our families (despite Jesus' abandonment of his own family).

Note how quickly, how effortlessly, and how predictably the preacher disposed of a story about Jesus and transformed it into a moralistic diatribe about us. Moving from a text that simply declares what Jesus did and, by implication, who Jesus is, the preacher turned to a moralistic rant on all the things that we need to do if we (lacking a living, active God) are to take charge of our lives and the world.

This is what Barth condemned as "religion," defined in *Romans* as "a vigorous and extensive attempt to humanize the divine, to make it a practical 'something,' for the benefit of those who cannot live with the Living God, and yet cannot live without God."[9]

Of course, most congregations that I know love such moralistic Deism. The subtext is always, "You are gods unto yourselves. Through this insight, this set of principles, this well-applied idea, you can save yourselves by yourselves." Whether the preacher is an alleged theological conservative or a would-be liberal, we're all Schleiermacherians now. Theology is reduced to anthropology because unlike Wesley, we're obsessed with ourselves rather than God. God is humanity spoken in a resonant, upbeat voice backed up with PowerPoint presentation. Our noble Arminianism really does degenerate into Pelagianism when the divine gift of divine-human synergism loses its divine initiation. My image of us United Methodists on Sunday morning is that we come to church with pencil and pad ready to get our assignments for the week: "This week, church, work on your sexism and racism, and be nice to salesclerks. Come back next week and I'll give you another assignment."

Wesley's much touted "Catholic spirit" was right to draw the line at extending the open hand of fellowship to Deists. Though Wesley might have been wrong in his belief in the reality of witches, he was right in his belief that the Deists' disbelief in witches was not to be trusted because of their truncated theological imaginations.[10]

Reaching out to speak to the world, we fell in facedown. Too troubled by our expectations of what our audience could and could not hear, we reduced the gospel to a set of sappy platitudes that anybody could accept and no sensitive, thinking person could resist. "Open minds, open hearts, open doors." Our testimony got reduced to whatever the market could bear. In the process of such "preaching," distinctive Christian speech was jettisoned, and the discourse of instrumental, utilitarian, therapeutic Deism is the dominant homiletic mode. Finney's pragmatism triumphs. A-theistic, simplified wisdom now dominates popular preaching (Warren's *Purpose Driven Life*) because preaching is no longer an expression of the peculiar actions of a triune God. People on top— well-fed, well-empowered people—always love Wisdom literature because of its lack of a God who either judges or redeems. Well-fixed people always want therapy more than salvation. We thus violated Barth's "first axiom of theology"—the first commandment, "thou shalt have no other gods before me."

Today the Methodist movement, at least in its North American and European vestiges, suffers from the debilitating effects of a truncated theology. We are attempting to revive a church on a too-thin description of God. Whereas Wesley's robust trinitarianism produced a vibrant, experimental, missional, adaptable ecclesiology that rejoiced in radical manifestations of the work of the Holy Spirit among ordinary people, today a virtually deistic view of God has rendered a dispirited, ossified ecclesia that in so many ways appears to be organized as a defense against the Holy Spirit. I marvel at Wesley's determination to deal with all organizational and missional questions from a theological point of view. Wesley was open to development and to change of the very structures he had created because he was determined to worship a living God whose perichoretic, trinitarian nature demanded a certain sort of institutional embodiment.

Sometimes as Methodists we need to be reminded of the vibrancy of Wesley's theology from surprising sources. Church growth guru Paul Borden, fresh from creating a virtually new, bourgeoning denomination among once dispirited American Baptists in California of all places, spoke with authority to our pastors recently. When asked, "What qualities do you most desire in pastors who are employed to start new congregations?" Borden replied, "They must be joyfully trinitarian and orthodox in their theology, stressing the redeeming work of God in Jesus Christ." I thought I was hearing Wesley.

Ecclesiologically, when the name *God* designates a stable, abstract essence rather than an active, reaching Trinity, then internal maintenance displaces external mission. The ministry that once was sent now becomes almost exclusively settled and parochial. The church that once planted congregations in thousands of places in order to follow Jesus everywhere is left behind by Jesus as we maintain and subsidize thousands of little churches that have long since ceased to bear any of the visible marks of the church and Jesus moves on to his next area of conquest.

Wesley's "conjunctive theology" (Ken Collins) in its complexity and tensive holding together of seemingly disparate emphases (knowledge and piety, sacramentalism and evangelism, faith and good works, justification and sanctification, personal holiness and social holiness, reason and enthusiasm, and so on) is just the sort of intellect that is produced by the worship of a complex God for whom Father, Son, and Holy Spirit, these three, are one.

If Wesley was right, then the best thing about John Wesley was the three-personed God who met Wesley at Aldersgate and elsewhere. As I read him, Wesley didn't so much love the poor as he loved the God who for our sakes became poor (Phil 2:6-10). He was not so much an organizational genius of the eighteenth century as a man who experienced firsthand the reality of the incarnation. Methodism, Wesley kept contending, was solely a miraculous work of God. He was not so much a great pastoral theologian as someone who was trying to figure out what had happened to scores of ordinary eighteenth-century English people after God had gotten to them in the miraculous movement called Methodism.

But if Wesley was right, then the trinitarian God may not be done with the Methodist movement yet; then God may find a way to meet us again in the present age. When we've got a resurrected Christ, we always have more future than past. God give us more theologians and fewer historians. Limp, static, inoffensive, and uninspired, merely contemporary views of God can be judged and corrected by our encounters with Wesley. When I read Wesley, I find that one of the Trinity's prominent attributes is not order, righteousness, or even love—it is momentum. Wesley's God is truly God in action, intruding everywhere. So whereas Dr. Whitehead emphasized, in his funeral sermon for Wesley, the pacifying, steadying effect upon the general population, I celebrate the potentially dislocating, disruptive effect of his robust view of a living God.

Thus Wesley may be able to rise up and speak to us yet, for he believed in an active, personal God who can kill and make alive, who refuses to be silenced, who loves to make a way to us when we presumed there was no way. If Wesley was right.

TRANSFORMING GRACE

My friend Stanley Hauerwas is fond of saying that when contemporary Anglicans talk about the incarnation, they don't know what they are talking about, and when Methodists speak today of grace, we know even less. Without the personality of a trinitarian God to give it specificity and content, "grace" becomes a vaguely benign spirit of divine beneficence toward an already benign humanity. Today, we're more inclined to "accept our humanity" than to worship a God who means radically to change us and to enlist us.

For Wesley, grace was the constant, moment-by-moment, active working of God in us that gives us a different life, indeed, a different world, than we would have had if God had left us alone. Without God we wretched sinners can do nothing, thought Wesley; with God we being-sanctified saints can do all things. Wesley took the Moravian one-time experience of spiritual enlightenment and made it a lifetime process of daily awakening to what grace can do among us: what we have learned from Randy Maddox to call "responsible grace." As early as 1733, Wesley preached the "one thing needful" as a soul that was being transformed by constant encounter with a living God.[11]

A transformed life is the anthropological result of a theological claim—"The best of all is God is with us." A trinitarian God never stops being Creator *pro nobis*, transforming everything that God touches. One of the most memorable impressions of Dick Heitzenrater's *Wesley and the People Called Methodists* is his depiction of the Spirit-induced heroism of ordinary Methodists. For Wesley, the transforming Holy Spirit was more than personal and subjective; it was corporate and ecclesial. Wesley delights to report the transformative work of the Holy Spirit on thousands of ordinary folk, even more than his delight in chronicling the results of the Holy Spirit on himself. Transformed lives confirmed Wesley's pneumatology.

At Aldersgate, Wesley experienced verification of the truth he had heretofore preached. As Heitzenrater puts it, at Aldersgate, "a long tradition of propositional certainty of faith met the power of a personal experience of the faith."[12]

Robert W. Cushman first told me that it was not so much Aldersgate that transformed Wesley but field preaching. Field preaching was against just about everything that Wesley had been educated to be for. I love Wesley's surprise at the response God gave to his field preaching. About the same time as Jonathan Edwards was marveling at *The Surprising Work of God in the Conversion of Many Hundred Souls in Northampton* (1737), Wesley was stunned by the effect of his field sermons at Bristol. When I read Wesley's *Sermons*, I share Wesley's shock that anybody was moved by his preaching. I find little to account for his homiletic effect other than a God who loves to raise the dead and to speak despite us.

As you know, Wesley's full embrace of both forgiveness and radical personal transformation sent Lutherans and Calvinists through the roof. On the cross, Jesus didn't just do something about our guilt; Jesus defeated the kingdom of Satan and established the kingdom of God; Jesus re-created the world and us, making us into a new people who had a fresh start in life. What Lutherans and Calvinists thought wrong was Wesley's extravagant assertion that something radical was done, is being done to sever our desires from their evil affections and to infuse us with robust craving to live a life of love toward God and neighbor.[13]

Don't you find it revealing that Wesley expended so much theological energy defending his notion that human beings could actually contribute something to their salvation? We must spend our time defending the divine side of divine/human synergy. It's not radical for us to think that we save ourselves by ourselves. What's radical is to assert a God who is able to work signs and wonders. In my efforts to prod denominational renewal, I would say that disbelief in a God who is able to do among us what God demands from us is the biggest impediment to renewal. The Enlightenment still holds our imaginations captive, and that captivity is killing us.

This Oxford Institute is concerned with matters of ecclesiology and missiology. May I begin the conversation by stating my belief that the God who transforms lives formed the basis of Wesley's ecclesiology? A sent ministry is what you get with a God who loves to go on "processions" (as the Fathers put the sending work of the Trinity). Why do we contemporary Wesleyans wring our hands over our alleged lack of an ecclesiology when, seen from one angle, that's all Wesley did—ecclesiology? His vision of God being so great and so lively as massively to transform the lives of ordinary eighteenth-century English people is an ecclesiology worth having—if Wesley was right.

Our great challenge in ecclesiology is that we've made salvation personal and subjective (William James has won). For Wesley salvation was always corporate. His elaborate, detailed attention to the life of the body is a rebuke to our religion-as-subjectivity. The wrong turn we took in frontier revivalism nurtured under William James, brought to flower in capitalism, is now running shamelessly among us as evangelicals wreak havoc in a church that once embodied holiness. Everything is reduced to "the message"—some trite expression suitable for a bumper sticker. Rather than transformation, preaching's goal becomes communication and acceptance of "the message" rather than life-changing encounter with Jesus the Messenger.

A best-selling book of 2006 says it all: *Leaving Church*.[14] Our God *dis*-incarnate determines that we all must disembody our faith and leave church in order to follow the governmentally approved *ordo salutis*—saving ourselves by descending ever deeper into our subjectivity. Because of our limp theology, our anthropology becomes too stable, and the purpose of our preaching is adjustment, confirmation rather than conversion. Preaching thus becomes another means of self-cultivation as well as a well-reasoned defense against true transformation.[15]

Wesley's ecclesiology has proved difficult for us heirs of Wesley to maintain, not because Wesley was too strict or too obsessive but because his was an ecclesiology that requires a certain sort of God to sustain it, namely, Wesley's lively trinitarian God of constant processions. Only a person who has a most extravagant notion of the miraculous power of God could devote nearly one-fourth of his first collection of *Sermons* to expositions of the Sermon on the Mount, taking with direct seriousness the ability of God to produce people who could live the lives assumed by the Sermon on the Mount.[16]

11   Heavenly Adam, life divine,
          Change my nature into thine:
          Move and spread throughout my soul,
          Actuate and fill the whole:
          Be it I no longer now,
          Living in the flesh, but thou.

12   Holy Ghost, no more delay,
          Come, and in thy temple stay;
          Now thy inward witness bear
          Strong and permanent, and clear;
          Spring of life, thyself impart,
          Rise eternal in my heart!

If Wesley was right, then we have some serious theological work to do. If Wesley was right about God, grace, mission, and the church, then we've got lots to talk about. Thank God we've got someone as interesting as Wesley to converse with.

Go with me to a dilapidated ex-warehouse that is today the Church of Innerchange at the *inter*change of two major interstates in Alabama. There, in a ministry that ranges from Bible study to paint ball tournaments, the Innerchange Church ministers to hard-living blue-collar people. I'm there on a Sunday.

"Before you speak, we'll show a video clip," the pastor told me. (I don't approve of multimedia homiletics, believing that preaching ought to be done the way Jesus did it—stand and deliver without aid of technology.)

So just before I speak, a voice on the video says, "Why do you come to the Church of Innerchange?"

A young African American man looks into the camera and says, "I met Pastor Mike. I told him I had a drug problem that I hadn't been able to shake. Pastor Mike told me, 'That's good. It's a sign that you know something's wrong in America. Lots of people aren't smart enough to know that God intends us for a better world. But drugs won't get you what you want. Let me show you Jesus.' I've been here ever since. One year, drug free. I couldn't have done it without Jesus and Innerchange."

A young woman, holding a small child, says, "One night my husband beat me so bad that I didn't leave the trailer for a week. I was so ashamed of how I looked. But the baby needed milk so I put on these sunglasses and a lot of makeup and went to the store. There, at the vegetable section, this woman comes up to me, takes off my glasses, and asks, 'What happened to you, honey?'

"I lied and told her I had a car accident. 'A man did this, didn't he?' she said. 'I know what that's like. Let me take you somewhere where you and your baby will be safe.' She brought me to Innerchange. This is the family I always knew God wanted me to have."

Through my own tears and inability to get up on my feet to preach, I mumbled, "So, Wesley was right!"

CHAPTER THREE

ECCLESIOLOGY FROM THE PERSPECTIVE OF SCRIPTURE IN WESLEYAN AND ASIAN CONTEXTS

Lung-kwong Lo

"Do Methodists Have a Doctrine of the Church?" is the title of Albert Outler's article that originated from his lecture in the 1962 Oxford Institute.[1] The Methodist Episcopal Church was organized in Baltimore in 1784, but the Wesleyan Methodists in Britain did not formally use the title "church" until 1897, despite the fact that the Wesleyan Conference urged parents to have their children baptized into "the church" in 1837.[2] The Methodist movement did not, in fact, intend to be a church and ended up becoming a separate church only through a series of unintended circumstances. This is one reason that Methodists have never claimed to be *the* church, as some other denominations do. Thus it is important and necessary for us as Methodists to continue our discussion of the doctrine of the church from biblical, historical, and contemporary perspectives in the present age of glocalization[3] so that we may serve it more diligently and with relevancy.

John Wesley understands Christianity as "scriptural Christianity"; therefore it is not only legitimate but also essential to study the doctrine of the church from a scriptural perspective. A full-scale and exhaustive discussion of the topic is beyond the scope of this essay. Some analysis, however, based on previous studies and from the perspective of my contexts, Wesleyan and Asian in general, Chinese in particular, may contribute to the ongoing conversation on the issues related to ecclesiology in the present age.

WESLEYAN AND ASIAN CONTEXTS OF THE PRESENT AGE

There are many ways of describing the present age. I prefer to use the term *glocalization* to describe the characteristics of both globalization and localization.[4] While globalization emphasizes the universality of the world and its interdependent effects on all people in different places, localization reminds us that the cultural, political, economic, and sociological differences of each community are still significant and essential for the construction of identity and meaning of life for everyone.

In my case, Wesleyan contexts are both universal and local. The Methodist Church, Hong Kong, inherited the traditions of the American Methodist Episcopal Mission (MEM), which sent missionaries to Fuzhou, China, in 1847,[5] and also the British Methodist Missionary Society, whose missionaries arrived in Hong Kong in 1851.[6] In 1975, we brought together both American and British Methodism into a united church. After the union, we decided to have a president instead of a bishop, which we had had before 1975.

In fact, the Methodist missionaries followed a wider missionary movement to China that was begun by the first Protestant missionary, Robert Morrison of Morpeth (near Newcastle, northeast England), sent by the London Missionary Society. He left England in January of 1807 and arrived at Macao on September 4 via New York.[7]

Being part of the world Methodist family, we acknowledge that we inherited the richness of American and British Methodism in spiritual and physical terms. However, our own contexts have also made us different. While the number of Methodists is declining in both American and British contexts, many Methodist churches in Asia are growing.[8] Asian Christians are, nevertheless, still a minority in the society. We live in a context of political struggle for a democracy that has to be developed from within our culture of respecting the status quo of the powerful. We also live in a context of economic growth so rapid that it has made the gap between the haves and have-nots even wider. Our traditional cultures are under threat by globalization. Religious pluralism is the reality of our everyday life. As a Hong Kong Chinese Methodist, I have to take the experiences of Chinese Christians into account.

When all missionaries, including Methodist, left mainland China after 1949, the system of denominations was abolished. The church that was established in 1950 emphasized "three-self principles." These principles were that churches should be self-governing, self-supporting, and self-propagating. Subsequently many missionaries adopted these principles to encourage churches in non-Western countries to develop from missionary-controlled churches to indigenous national churches.[9] The church in China experienced a trial by fire during the Cultural Revolution (1966–76).[10] However, the number of Christians did not decrease but increased rapidly during and following that period. The number in 1997 had increased fifteenfold compared to the number in 1949, when there were not more than 700,000. In 2006, the number of Protestants in China was not less than 20 million.[11]

Thus this essay will discuss ecclesiology from the perspective of Scripture with these contexts in mind.

SCRIPTURAL PERSPECTIVES ON CHURCH

In his famous book *Images of the Church in the New Testament*,[12] Paul Minear identifies thirty-two metaphors and pictures as minor images of the church in the New Testament. Then he groups another sixty-four metaphors into four major images: the people of God, the new creation, the fellowship in faith, and the body of Christ. Minear's study is probably still the most comprehensive work on how "the New Testament writers thought and spoke about the church."[13] However, Minear's study originated from the Theological Commission on Christ and the Church, under the auspices of the Faith and Order Commission of WCC in 1954. Its concern, therefore, is "within the context of the Faith and Order Movement" with the unity of the church in mind. The study and those images of the church are not discussed in the context of mission, even though Minear acknowledges the importance of mission. It "is the word that spans the total distance between God and the world's salvation. The whole dynamic of the church's life may be conveyed by this single word."[14] In fact, early Christianity was consciously and deliberately a missionary movement. Mission was essential for its establishment and maintenance.

The context of mission as the prior context for our understanding of the doctrines of the church is essential not only to the early church but also to the contemporary church. Emil Brunner has rightly emphasized that "the church exists by mission, just as fire exists by burning; where there is no mission, there is no church."[15] According to our experiences in Asia, Brunner's statement is true. Furthermore, according to Outler, "Wesley defined the church as *act*, as mission, as the enterprise of saving and maturing souls in the Christian life."[16] Methodism, at its best, has also seen the structure of the church as determined by the needs of Christian mission.[17] Thus, to discuss our understanding of church in the context of mission is not only biblical but also consistent with the Wesleyan tradition and also true to the experiences of Asian Christians.

In this essay, Minear's images of "the people of God" will be modified to "the *minjung*[18] of God," "the body of Christ" to "Word in flesh." Church as "the community of disciples" will be substituted for "the fellowship of faith," and "the temple of Holy Spirit" will replace "the new creation."

The Greek word for church is *ekklesia*, derived from the verb *ekkaleo* (called out), which originally referred to the summons for an army to assemble. From the fifth century B.C.E. onward the word is used to denote the popular assembly of the competent, full citizens of the city (*polis*), which met at regular intervals to make fundamental political and judicial decisions (see Acts 19:32, 39, 41).[19] It is noteworthy that the word always retained its reference to the assembly of the *polis* as a political phenomenon, except in two cases. It was not used for guilds or religious societies.[20]

Moreover, in the Septuagint (LXX), *ekklesia* is used to translate the Hebrew term *qahal* some seventy-three times out of a total of one hundred twenty-three occurrences to denote "assembly, convocation, and congregation" or any group of people brought together.[21] It was used quite frequently to denote the people of Israel gathered together to hear God's Law at Sinai (Deut. 5:22; 9:10; 10:4) or from the mouth of Joshua (Josh. 8:35), or on other religious occasions (Num. 15:15). It could be used to represent Israel as a whole, even when it was not actually gathered in an assembly (Lev. 16:17). There are also a number of references to the "assembly of YHWH" (Num. 16:3; 20:4; Deut. 23:1-8; 1 Chron. 28:8; Neh. 13:1; Lam. 1:10; Mic. 2:5; see "the assembly of the people of God" in Judg. 20:2). However, the word is never used to render another Hebrew word, *edah*, which also means "congregation," but in the sense of the national unity of the people.[22] The word *sunagoge*, which is used by Jews to denote their communities, has been used to translate both *qahal* (thirty-five times) and *edah* (one hundred thirty times).[23] This may be one of the essential reasons behind the earliest followers of Christ using *ekklesia* to denote the church as a religious gathering of a new group of people, that is, to distinguish themselves from both Greco-Roman religious associations and Jewish synagogues of their time.

In the New Testament, *ekklesia* appears only three times in two verses of the Gospel of Matthew (16:18; and twice in 18:17) and not at all in the other canonical Gospels. However, it occurs one hundred fourteen times in the New Testament; sixty-two instances are in the Pauline letters (five in Romans; twenty-two in 1 Corinthians; nine in 2 Corinthians; three in Galatians; nine in Ephesians; two in Philippians; four in Colossians; two each in 1 and 2 Thessalonians; three in 1 Timothy; one in Philemon); another twenty-three in Acts; twenty in Revelation; and six in non-Pauline letters. Paul must be among the earliest to use the word to shape the concept of church as the congregation of God (*ekklesia tou theou*) in 1 Thess. 2:14; 2 Thess. 1:4; 1 Cor. 1:2; 10:32; 11:22; 15:9; 2 Cor. 1:1; Gal. 1:13; Phil. 3:6; also Acts 20:28; *ekklesia tou christou* only in Rom. 16:16; and *ekklesia en christo* only in Gal. 1:22), which corresponds with *qahal* (YHWH),[24] a counterpart of the Sinai congregation (see 1 Cor. 10:1-5; Heb. 12:18-24). In other words, the idea of "congregation/people of God"[25] in the Old Testament is not restricted to old Israel but is now used to identify the New Testament congregation/people of God as well. In the early church, *ekklesia* could refer to the entire community of followers of Christ (Matt. 16:18; 1 Cor. 12:28; Acts

20:28) and also, especially in the plural (*ekklesiai*), to communities of followers in a specific location (Matt. 18:17; 1 Thess. 1:1; 2 Thess. 1:4; 2:14; 1 Cor. 1:2; 7:17; 11:16; 14:33, 34; 16:1, 19; 2 Cor. 1:1; 8:1, 19, 23, 24; 11:8, 28; 12:13; Gal. 1:2, 22; Rom. 16:4; and house church in Rom. 16:5). The church as the total community is not a mere aggregate of individual congregations; rather, the local church is the universal church in its local manifestation.[26]

From the above brief account of the meaning of *ekklesia*, I summarize as follows:

1. The term has its root in the gathering of qualified citizens of the polis who are called out to make communal decisions. In other words, the citizens gathered were called to be accountable to one another with commitment.
2. The term has its root also in the LXX to indicate the assembly of the people of God in the Old Testament. This indicates that the church inherits and shares the spiritual richness of Israel, and the term also represents a dynamic gathering rather than a static organization.
3. Early Christians use it to identify themselves in order to distinguish themselves from both Greco-Roman and Jewish associations. The church is both in continuity and in discontinuity with the Jewish communities of its time.
4. The term is used to denote both local congregations and a total entity. In other words, it also refers to an implicit tension between local and universal.

These characteristics of *ekklesia* are echoed in the early stages of the Methodist movement, for example:

1. Methodism had been a movement inside the Church of England for not less than a hundred years by the time it became a distinctive church in Britain. The Methodist Church has a nuanced relationship of continuity and discontinuity with the Church of England.[27] It is obvious that The Methodist Church has inherited the traditions of the Church of England, especially those that distinguish its doctrines, worship, and sacraments.[28]
2. The precise origins of the identity of the term *Methodist* are unclear. Wesley's followers were vaguely identified as "the

people called Methodist." The early Methodists were a fluid group of people; many were from the poorest part of the population with distinctive characteristics.[29]

3. The early Methodists were grouped into classes that emphasized a particular form of *discipline* or accountability as a distinct element of Christian fellowship. This discipline not only made Methodism distinctive but also, in fact, helped the rapid expansion of Methodism in America.

4. The Methodist Church has been organized into conferences, districts, and circuits since its early days. The distinctive work of the Methodist office of elders is the *itinerant* ministry. Basically, the accountability of the elders goes to the conference (or bishops in the United States) first, then the local churches. The ecclesiology of The Methodist Church accepts that the conference represents the connectedness of the total entity of The Methodist Church; all local Methodist churches share the burdens and resources together through the connection of the conference.[30] Local Methodist churches are The Methodist Church in its local manifestation. The Methodist Church is a church of *unity* in *diversity*.[31] The itinerancy of The Methodist Church is *centralized* and yet *decentralized (localized)*, which has also contributed to the expansion of Methodism in many places, especially in the expanding American frontier in the 1800s.[32]

Nevertheless, in discussing the use of the phrase "the people of God" as an image of the church, Minear has rightly pointed out that "the modern reader . . . is in the habit of using the word 'people' in the most casual and vague way to indicate human beings in general."[33] *People* becomes a mass of people without faces.

In the LXX, the word *laos* (people) occurs about two thousand times. It often signifies the people in contrast to the ruler or ruling class (see Gen. 41:40; 47:21; Exod. 1:22; Jer. 23:34), and in the overwhelming majority of cases is a translation of the Hebrew *cam* and means Israel as the chosen people of God. About ten times, Israel is called the "people of YHWH"; in another three hundred cases there are forms with a pronominal suffix (e.g., *cammi*, "my people"), where the suffix refers to YHWH.[34] In the New Testament, *laos* occurs one hundred forty-one times, eighty-four being in

Luke–Acts and fourteen in Matthew, twelve in Pauline letters, thirteen in Hebrews, and nine in Revelation. It may be affected by LXX that *laos* often follows a previous reference to *ochlos* (crowd) and carries the same meaning (e.g., Luke 7:24, 29; 8:42, 47; see also Matt. 27:25-26; Mark 14:2), or stands instead of *ochlos* in a parallel passage (e.g., Luke 19:48; see Mark 11:18; Luke 20:45; Matt. 23:1). When *laos* is used on its own, it can also mean crowd, the common people (Luke 1:10; 7:1; 20:1, 9; Acts 2:47).

As in the LXX, *laos* can mean the people in contrast to the ruling classes (Luke 22:2; 23:5; Acts 6:2), or in a cultic setting the broad mass of people as opposed to the priest (Heb. 5:3; 7:27), or again, the ordinary people as opposed to the few witnesses of the resurrection (Acts 10:41; 13:31). Furthermore, Israel is described as the *laos* (the *laos Israel*, Acts 4:10; 13:17; *houtos ho laos*, "this people," in Old Testament quotations at Matt. 13:15 [Isa. 6:10]; 15:8 [Isa. 29:13]; Acts 28:26-28 [Isa. 6:9-10]; Rom. 9:25-26 [Hos. 2:23; 1:10]; 10:21 [Isa. 65:2]; 11:2 [1 Sam. 12:22; Ps. 94:14; and Lam. 3:31]; 15:10-11 [Deut. 32:43]; 1 Cor. 10:7 [Exod. 32:6]; 14:21 [Isa. 28:11-12]; 2 Cor. 6:16 [Lev. 26:12; Exod. 29:45; Ezra 37:27; Jer. 31:1]). In Hebrews, especially, statements of the Old Testament cultus, seen as types of Christ, are transferred to the church.[35] Similarly, in 1 Peter 2:9 (Exod. 19:5-6) and in Revelation 18:4 (see Jer. 51:45) and 21:3 (see Zech. 2:10; Ezek. 37:27), the Old Testament passages are applied to the church as the new people of God (*laos theou*).[36]

When we use the image of church as "the people of God," the first question we should ask is, *Who are the people?* As for the "people" of God in the Old Testament, their characteristics were specific and clear. They were the descendants of a wandering Aramean (Deut. 26:5), slaves in Egypt, saved by the covenant God who led them through the wilderness and toward the promised land (Exod. 6:1-8; 19:4-6; Deut. 26:6-8). However, when we define the church as people of God, we are seldom aware of the fact that worldwide Christianity has a greater number of adherents than any other religion, with the majority of them residing in politically and economically powerful countries in the West.[37] National churches in many European countries represent colonial and imperialistic powers that invaded many countries in Africa and Asia in the eighteenth and nineteenth centuries. Some "Christian" political leaders like to use religious slogans and terms to propagate their political ideologies. In other words, in modern times, Christians in many countries are the majority identified with the ruling power, not with the common people.

Though the name "Methodist" has been used to identify the followers of John Wesley or converts enrolled in Wesleyan Methodist Societies, which originated at Oxford in the year 1729, John Wesley did not really like the name and rarely used it without careful qualification.[38] He preferred to use the long name of "the people called Methodist." The Methodist movement started among the university students of Oxford, but many of the people who later joined were poor, people from the grassroots of society, or marginalized people, including widows, orphans, prisoners, and coal miners.[39]

A BBC television series, broadcast in 1995–96, named the twentieth century as the "people's century."[40] For Americans, the ideal of a government "of the people, by the people, for the people" was spelled out in the previous century in President Lincoln's 1863 Gettysburg Address. This understanding sees "people" as all the citizens of the nation and thus has become an ideal for many people in the world.

In Asian contexts, "people" represented those who are powerless and had always been treated as the objects, not the subjects, of history. The Communist parties of China, North Korea, and Vietnam promoted the so-called people's movement in their revolutions and national buildings. They called their government the People's Republic. The word *people* has become a Communist word. For them, *people* means the proletariat. However, an understanding of people's power that bears no relationship to communism has exerted great influence of late in some Asian countries and regions, including the Philippines (1986), mainland China (1989), and even Hong Kong (2003). *People* in Asia is a dangerous and politically sensitive term for powerless people. In spite of this connotation, Korean theologians coined their contextual theology as *minjung* (people) theology in the 1980s.

One of the forerunners of *minjung* theology, David Kwang-sun Suh, says,

> *Minjung* is a term which grew out of the Christian experiences in the political struggle for justice over the last ten or more years. Theology

of *minjung* or *minjung* theology is an accumulation and articulation of theological reflections on the political experiences of Christian students, laborers, the press, professors, farmers, writers, and intellectuals as well as theologians in Korea in the 1970s. It is a theology of the oppressed in the Korean political situation, a theological response to the oppressors, and it is the response of the oppressed to the Korean church and its mission. . . . It was a search for a contextual theology in Asia.[41]

In fact, the search has not been completed; different kinds and forms of *minjung* theology are still developing in different parts of Asia.[42] In this context, *minjung* as "people" transcends the boundaries of social classes and backgrounds but represents people who are aware of and who experience different kinds of oppression in their life situations. The struggle for an equal share of love, justice, and power in society is the direction of their endeavor. The main concern is how to let "people" be the subjects, rather than objects, of history. Thus, to understand the church as "*minjung*/people" of God, composed of those called by God, identifies the "church" with the *minjung* of society and those whose lives find direction under God's lordship. This context of mission is vital for our understanding of ecclesiology in Asian contexts.

CHURCH AS THE CONGREGATION IN THE WILDERNESS (ACTS 7:38)

In our discussion of the term *ekklesia*, I indicated that Paul probably was one of the earliest followers to shape the concept of church as the congregation of God in association with the *qahal* counterpart of the Sinai congregation. According to Davies and Allison, the connection of church and the congregation of God in the Old Testament is also perceived in the Gospel of Matthew.[43] There are numerous parallels between Jesus and Moses in Matthew, suggesting that the church had its origin in a new exodus.[44] However, the image of the church as "the congregation in the wilderness" (Acts 7:38) is not found in Minear's book (Acts 7:38 is not even in the index).[45] In fact, it does not attract the attention of many scholars.[46] Nevertheless, C. K. Barrett has rightly pointed out that "it is very doubtful whether Luke wrote, or any early Christian read, this verse without thinking of the Christian *ekklesia*, of which he would see a foreshadowing in the ancient people of God."[47]

In Acts, *ekklesia* occurs twenty-three times: sixteen times in Acts 1–15 (omitting the problematic addition in 2:47),[48] and seven times in Acts 16–28. Three of the latter occurrences (19:32, 39, 41) clearly denote the assembly of citizens as the *polis* of Ephesus but not the church. The understanding of the term *ekklesia* in Acts, the only New Testament book that gives an account of the birth of the church at Pentecost (chap. 2) and also describes the life of the early church (2:42-47; 4:32-35), is crucial for our discussion. Among the twenty relevant occurrences, eight denote the community in Jerusalem (5:11; 8:1, 3; 11:22; 12:5; 15:4, 22; 18:22). As the gospel spread from Jerusalem into the world, this term came to be applied to other local Christian groups, such as Antioch with four occurrences (11:26; 13:1; 14:27; 15:3) and Ephesus with one (20:17). The other three denote the group of converts resulting from Paul's first missionary journey (14:23; 16:5), and of these, one denotes those in Syria and Cilicia (15:41). In Acts 9:31 the term is used to refer to the church through the whole of Judea and Galilee and Samaria. However, in 20:28 the term refers to the church of God, obtained by the blood of God's own Son. Barrett suggests that *ekklesia* is here "the worldwide company of the redeemed, *ecclesia catholica*."[49]

Among these twenty occurrences, only the reference occurring in 7:38 is related directly to the people of God in the Old Testament. In addition, however, Stephen's sermon (7:2-51) elicits a number of corollaries drawn from the phrase "congregation in the wilderness" that allude to the close relationship between the early Christians' understanding of church and the Old Testament people of God:

1. The image depicts a community of people who are helpless, poor, isolated, and in a quest for their future. They are on their own and can do nothing but depend on God for their living and future. Their destiny is tied up together. They are bound to seek their future and destiny as a community. In other words, they are a congregation of life and death. No individuals can survive if they leave the congregation.

2. In Stephen's speech, Moses is the most important figure (vv. 20-44 among fifty-three verses). Apparently, the rejection of Moses by his people and his vindication by God suggest to Stephen a foreshadowing of the rejection and vindication of Jesus (Acts 2:22-23; 3:12-15; 4:10-11; 5:28-32).[50] Moses prophesied the coming of a prophet like himself (v. 37; see 3:22). The parallel of Moses and Jesus is clearly indicated in the Gospel of Matthew as referred to above. In the speech, the exodus is the paradigm adopted to indicate the mission of Jesus.

3. The promise given to Abraham, we are reminded, is fulfilled in the time of Moses (7:17), thereby modeling the coming of Jesus as the new Moses.

4. Moses was depicted as "the one who was in the congregation in the wilderness with the angel who spoke to him at Mount Sinai, and with our ancestors; and he received living oracles to give to us" (v. 38). This description likely refers to the transfiguration of Jesus (Luke 9:28-34) and the first preaching of Jesus according to the Gospel of Luke (4:16-21).

5. In the speech, Stephen critiques not the law but the temple alone (vv. 46-50).[51] He seems to indicate that the "tent of testimony in the wilderness" (v. 44) and "congregation in the wilderness" are the patterns closer to God's expectation than the temple. The "congregation in the wilderness" suggests the movement of people rather than a static institution like the temple. This understanding is in line with the concept of *ekklesia* in the early church.

6. The "congregation in the wilderness" is the people of God formed by God's mighty acts performed in Egypt, and this congregation is moving from Egypt to the promised land under the direction of God.[52] However, sometime during their journey they grow rebellious (groaning) and are influenced by the religions of neighboring peoples (worshiping alien gods). This image parallels the church in the New Testament, in that, by the shedding of Christ's blood, God formed and set apart a people, racially and culturally mixed. They faced various temptations from Greco-Roman society. They also became a congregation living among alien peoples and religions rather than a static institution.

John Wesley's sermon "The Wilderness State" (1760), which alludes to the image of Israel in the wilderness, argues that grumbling against God is indicative of the ultimate spiritual problem: lost faith in Christ.[53] In his sermons "Wandering Thoughts" (1762) and "Heaviness through Multifold Temptations" (1760), he identifies and categorizes a range of spiritual problems or illnesses that the believer might face in the quest of sanctification: temptation, fear, false security, boasting of religious accomplishments, forms of religious depression. Sanctification is not a lonely quest. It is a quest undertaken in company, with the whole system of Methodist class meetings, societies, bands, and other groupings as means to assist the seeker and the believer.[54] In other words, it is not an individual quest but is carried out by a congregation, bound together, moving toward their communal destiny like the "congregation in the wilderness." Moreover, in the Wesleyan pattern, sanctification is "a process in which believers seek the sanctification of the world around them. John Wesley himself encouraged the Methodists to take part in a wide range of *movements* for the betterment of social conditions."[55] After Wesley's time, Methodists involved themselves in efforts to improve conditions for laborers, women, and children; to end gambling; to control consumption of alcohol; to combat racism; to act against nuclear proliferation; and to respond to the issues of global warming in the present age.

The image of the "congregation in the wilderness" is especially valuable for Asian Christians—we live as a minority in a multireligious and multicultural world—as we seek an understanding of the doctrine of the church. The "congregation in the wilderness" correlates with the *minjung* of the society; and this image raises the awareness of the *minjung* to our own journey in the wilderness, which is unfriendly and even hostile to our movement toward the promised land of love, justice, and equity. The church in Asia bears the burdens and richness of the missionary history of the past. We face complaints, accusations, and challenges from our members and also countrypeople. We search out our own identity and destiny. We will learn how to be bound together as a church to face many difficult challenges. Our major challenge is the tension between the Christian tradition and our cultures: the issue of religious syncretism (an issue of the relation of gospel and religions) and disorientation from our national identity (an issue of gospel and cultures).[56]

CHURCH AS THE COMMUNITY OF DISCIPLES (THE FELLOWSHIP IN FAITH)

The image of the church as "the fellowship in faith" suggested by Minear is not only too general, but it is also not a phrase used in the New Testament, although "the faithful" occurs.[57] Therefore, I suggest combining the images of "disciples"[58] and the "witnessing community"[59] to become "the community of disciples" as a major image of the church.

As mentioned above, other than in the Gospel of Matthew, the term *ekklesia* does not appear in the canonical Gospels. The church, however, begins in the Gospels with Jesus' followers, specifically those referred to as disciples. Jesus called a group of "twelve" disciples as a core to accompany him. The "twelve" and "disciples" seem to be identical in Matthew 10:1 and Mark 3:14; nevertheless, the term *mathetes* (disciple) does not occur in Luke 10:1-20, in which seventy (-two) were also appointed by Jesus and sent to the same ministry as the "twelve" (9:1-6; see Matt. 9:37-38; 10:5-15, 40; 11:21-23; Mark 6:7-13).[60] Mark gives evidence of disciples with Jesus before the "twelve" were chosen (2:15, 16, 18, 23; 3:7, 9; 4:34; 5:31; 6:1); this implies that there was an undefined group of disciples outside the circle of the "twelve."[61] Matthew specifically speaks of them (8:19, 21) and alludes to a wider circle of disciples (10:24-25, 42). He even acknowledges through the verb *matheteuo* the discipleship of Joseph of Arimathea (Matt. 27:57). Luke indicates that Jesus chose the "twelve" from among a much larger number of disciples (Luke 6:13, 17). In the Gospels, one of the tasks of Jesus was to call people to follow him (Matt. 8:18-22; 19:16-22; Mark 10:17-31; Luke 9:57-62; 18:18-30), and he also told those surrounding him or traveling with him that if they did not commit themselves, they could not be his disciples (Luke 14:25-33; see Matt. 10:37-38).

In Acts 1:21-26, the disciples, now numbering eleven (apostles, 1:26) after the death of Judas, have to choose "one of the men who have accompanied us during all the time that the Lord Jesus went in and out among us, beginning from the baptism of John until the day when he was taken up from us—one of these must become a witness with us to his resurrection . . . to take the place in this ministry and apostleship." John further suggests that many disciples of Jesus left him after hearing his teaching (John 6:60-69); but the twelve stayed on.[62] In 1 Corinthians 15:3-8, Paul mentions that when Jesus was raised from the dead, he appeared to Peter, the twelve, and then five hundred brothers, James and all the apostles, and then himself. The above evidence points to the existence of a community of disciples, not only the "twelve," who were followers of Jesus.

In the New Testament, all 261 references to *mathetes* are found in the Gospels and Acts but primarily in the Gospels; only 10 percent of the references occur in Acts. The other word, *akolouthein* (to walk behind, to follow), is also frequently used in the New Testament as a specialized term for following Jesus. Among the ninety occurrences, seventy are found in the Gospels, the rest in Acts (four times), Revelation (six times), and 1 Corinthians (once). This also indicates that discipleship is closely associated with Jesus himself. In Matthew 28:16-20, the Great Commission, the eleven disciples were sent to make disciples among all nations. And it was in Antioch that the disciples were first called "Christians" (Acts 11:26). In other words, discipleship is important not only in the time of Jesus but also from the early church onward. Luke-Acts is the bridge between the time of the Gospels and the early church.[63] Even though the familiar use of *ekklesia* does not exist in the time of Jesus, the community of disciples is the prototype of it. Thus the image of the community of disciples is appropriately considered a major image of the church. Although Minear does not list this image in his four primary images, he acknowledges, "Each Gospel pericope became a paradigm with a message for the church because each Christian had inherited a relationship to Jesus similar to that of James and John and the others."[64]

The essentials needed to participate in the community of Jesus' disciples have been clearly spelled out in the Gospels; they could be summarized as follows:

1. Jesus' calling, and not one's motivation, initiates discipleship.[65] Jesus confronts those he encounters—in passing, in shared travels, or in sustained relationships—demanding total submission of their lives to him. The sense of calling and the recognition of the lordship of Jesus are essential to discipleship.

2. The conditions of following him are clear. Jesus demands a total break with the past, including the leaving of families and vocations (e.g., Mark 1:16-20; 2:14; Matt. 8:21-22; Luke 14:25-27).

3. Following Jesus demands a radical renunciation of control over one's possessions, requiring a sharing with poor persons rather than an increase in acquisitions (Mark 10:21; Matt. 19:21; Luke 18:22).

4. Discipleship also demands denial of oneself in order to take up the cross and follow Jesus. This means to follow Jesus to the death (Mark 8:34-35; Matt. 10:38-39; 16:24-25; Luke 9:23-24).

5. Discipleship includes the expectation that the disciple will serve rather than be served (Mark 10:41-45; Matt. 24–28).

6. Discipleship also means entering into a lifelong relationship with Jesus (Mark 3:14); that is, disciples are to be in union with Jesus as the branches are with the vine (John 15:1-5; 17:20-26).

7. Disciples are not only called to follow Jesus but are also commissioned to proclaim the gospel (Mark 3:14), to be his witnesses (Acts 1:6-8), and also to exercise his power (Matt. 9:37-38; 10:5-15, 40; 11:21-23; 28:18-20; Mark 6:7-13; Luke 9:1-6).[66] Jesus prayed for his disciples and sent them out, as he had been sent by God (John 17:18; 21:22).

8. Jesus' mission is to bring the kingdom of God into this world; his disciples also participate in this kingdom mission.[67]

9. Disciples are called as individuals[68] but follow Jesus only communally. In other words, Jesus calls individuals to a community with Jesus as the Master.[69]

The above findings are most significant for our Wesleyan traditions. According to Ted Campbell, "Disciplined accountability in small groups has been a distinctly Methodist nuance of the understanding of 'church,' and the original stress of the Methodist *Discipline* was on the distinct form of accountable discipleship."[70] This had in fact made the Methodist movement an alternative account of Christian fellowship within the Church of England.

In the Asian context, especially in China, understanding and experiencing the meaning of discipleship were of utmost importance for the rooting and growing of the church from its inception. Missionaries came to China in the nineteenth century when China was not yet ready to be opened to the world. The blood of the missionaries was the seed of the church just as truly as was that of the martyrs for the early church. The growing number of Christians in mainland China during the Cultural Revolution witnesses to this truth: Jesus' call to discipleship is costly but shows its power when the situation seems to make people feel powerless. In fact, this was also the experience of the people who participated in the independence movements in many Asian countries. The cost of life is paid for something more valuable than life. As Bonhoeffer said: "When Christ calls a man, he bids him come and die."[71] And as Confucius said, "One could die just as light as a feather, but one could die as heavy as Taishan" (a famous big mountain in northeast China near the native county of Confucius).[72] So, dying for Christ gives value to one's life. This remains true for the present age: "Cheap grace is the deadly enemy of our Church."[73] Only an understanding of grace as responsible grace is a blessing to the church. The understanding of the church as a community of disciples willing to die for Jesus is crucial in Asian contexts.

CHURCH AS THE WORD IN FLESH (THE BODY OF CHRIST)

The exact phrase "the body of Christ" occurs only four times in the Pauline letters (*to soma tou Christou*: Rom. 7:4; 1 Cor. 10:16; Eph. 4:12; *soma Christou*: 1 Cor. 12:27). However, there are seventeen other equivalent expressions, such as "the cup of the Lord" (1 Cor. 11:27); "his fleshly body" (Col. 1:22); "his body of glory" (Phil. 3:21); "his body" (Eph. 1:23; 5:30; Col. 1:24); "my body" (1 Cor. 11:24); "the body" (1 Cor. 11:29; Eph. 5:23; Col. 1:18; 2:19); and "one body" (Rom. 12:5; 1 Cor. 10:17; 12:13; Eph. 2:16; 4:4;

Col. 3:15). Among them, only two passages in Colossians directly relate "the body" (1:18) and "his body" (1:24) to the church. All other occurrences do not express directly that the church is the body of Christ. However, there is no doubt that the image of the body is the dominant theological image in Pauline ecclesiology.

For Paul, this image is mainly used in (1) sacramental language, that is, the broken bread (1 Cor. 10–11, especially 10:16-17; 11:24-29),[74] (2) to denote the unity of a community despite the diversity of its members, that is, church (Rom. 12:4, 5; 1 Cor. 12:14-26; Col. 2:19; Eph. 4:11-16), and (3) to denote the unity of Christ as the head of the church and church as the body of Christ (Col. 1:18; see 1 Cor. 12:13).[75]

In the Christian tradition it has been customary to speak of the church as the extension of the incarnation.[76] This has often led to the mistake of extending this understanding of church to make church identical with the kingdom of God on earth. However, Bonhoeffer says: "The Body of Christ takes up physical space on earth. That is a consequence of the Incarnation,"[77] and J. A. T. Robinson also traces a connection between John 1:14, 16 and Colossians 1:19. The fullness with which Christ is filled by God is now filling those who are "in Him."[78] In recent discussions of the understanding of church, Graham Ward, a young representative of radical orthodoxy, also suggests that there is a relationship between the body of Christ and the incarnation in the series of events of the earthly Jesus, including transfiguration, Eucharist, death, resurrection, and ascension.[79] Thus it is better to see the church metaphorically as the Word in flesh than to see the church, the body of Christ, as the extension of incarnation.

The choice of using the phrase "Word in flesh" instead of "Word became flesh" is intended to indicate that the church is not the extension of incarnation but the concrete expression of incarnation in our present age. The invisible becomes visible;[80] the abstract becomes concrete. The church should understand itself as the witness of Jesus Christ's continued presence in the world. We are not Jesus Christ himself, but we are by God's grace sent by him to do what he would do and even greater works (John 14:12). For he who comes from God (see 1 Cor. 8:6; 2 Cor. 8:9; Phil. 2:6; Eph. 1:4; Col. 1:16; John 1:1-18; Heb. 1:1-4) accepts humanity by taking upon himself our human nature, "sinful flesh" (Rom. 8:3-4), and human form (Gal. 4:4; Phil. 2:6-8).[81] By its very nature, the church is not a building, not an organization, not a static established institution, but the body of Christ signifying that Jesus is still living among us. So the body of Christ exists as a people's movement, as a moving congregation in the wilderness heading toward the promised land, a community of disciples who are willing and ready to follow Jesus unto death. The church exists only if it is a living entity, living among *minjung* full of grace and truth as Jesus Christ is living in this world. Because Jesus Christ is risen and ascended to heaven, it is the church in following Christ that acts with him to bring grace and truth to the world (John 1:14) and to witness his presence in the world.

The church not only exists by mission but is by nature missionary. The very existence of the church is based on the calling of Christ, and it is sent into the world by Christ (John 17:18; 21:22). From the very beginning, the zeal of preaching the gospel created the Methodist movement. If Methodism cannot maintain this missionary zeal, Methodism will not continue to exist.

The church in Asia has been understood variously as imperialist invaders, colonists, capitalists, preachers, educators, medical doctors, social workers, and activists. Asians are in general pragmatic people, looking for actions rather than words. Thus the church seen as the Word in flesh indicates that the Word should be manifested by the church in proclamation as well as service-in-action. The concept of church as Word in flesh is therefore essential for furthering an Asian understanding of Christianity and the church.

CHURCH AS THE TEMPLE OF THE HOLY SPIRIT (EPHESIANS 2:22)

Among the ninety-six images of the church provided by Minear, only two are related to the Holy Spirit: "communion in the Holy Spirit" and "spiritual body" (1 Cor. 15). The phrase "communion in the Holy Spirit" does not exist in the New Testament, and it is doubtful whether we should consider the image of "spiritual body" to be directly related to the church. In 1 Corinthians 15, the issues discussed relate not so much to the understanding of the church as to the bodily resurrection of the dead and the form of the bodies that the dead will take when they rise from the tomb.[82] However, the position and the role of the Holy Spirit are essential in our understanding of the church.

When we see the church as "the temple of the Holy Spirit," it seems quite contradictory. Our image of temple would be the static building that stood in Jerusalem, while the Holy Spirit signifies movement and power. Nevertheless, the combination of these two is not only supported by the New Testament; it is also a very important image of the church.

In Acts, the first congregation of God is gathered after Peter's speech on the day of Pentecost. The pouring out of the Holy Spirit and fire upon all flesh in fulfillment of Joel's prophecy stresses the dependence of the church upon this gift of God for its unity, its mission, its power, and its worship.[83] Paul says, "Do you not know that you are God's temple and that God's Spirit dwells in you?" (1 Cor. 3:16; see 1 Cor. 3:17; 6:19-20; 2 Cor. 6:16–7:1). Paul's use of the temple (naos) to denote the church demonstrates that, as a Jew, he believes that the church is the dwelling place of God. In 2 Corinthians 6:16-18, Paul quotes several Old Testament passages in catena form[84] to emphasize that the church is also the people of God in continuity with the people of God in the Old Testament. Furthermore, the temple in Jerusalem is the place for offering sacrifice. However, for Paul, there is no sacrifice in this temple; the sacrifice is the living sacrifice of our bodies (Rom. 12:1-2) with the aroma of Christ (2 Cor. 2:15).[85] The sacrificial nature of Christian life and practice, the process of sanctification, is in the mind of Paul.[86] It is noteworthy that for Paul, the temple is the temple of God or God's Spirit and never the temple of Christ. However, the relationship of Christ to the temple is found in the metaphor of church as a house (oikodome) or temple under construction with Christ as the foundation (1 Cor. 3:11) and the cornerstone (Eph. 2:20),[87] while Paul is a founder and builder (1 Cor. 3:9-10; 2 Cor. 10:8; 12:19; 13:10; Rom. 15:20). The readers of Paul's letters are reassured that what they do helps build one another up toward the ideal of a community whose mutual concern wholly expresses the spirit and love of Christ (Rom. 14:17-19; 15:2; 1 Cor. 10:24;

Eph. 4:29; Phil. 2:4; 1 Thess. 5:11).[88] The image of the temple is also connected to the image of the body (*soma*) of individuals in 1 Corinthians 6:19 and 2 Corinthians 7:1.

In Ephesians 2:20-22, the image of church as the temple is clearly used for doctrinal instruction, and the image is fused with that of the building. Following the discussion in the preceding verses (vv. 11-19), the image denotes that the temple is not only for the Jews but also for the Gentiles. This temple is being built for all people, including those considered strangers and aliens in the past.

In 1 Peter 2:4-10, the church of the New Testament is understood as inheriting the promises, enjoying the privileges, and conducting the function of the people of God of the Old Testament. The titles for Israel as used in Exodus 19:5-6 are now used for the church as well. The "spiritual house" with Jesus Christ as the cornerstone laid by God at Zion (vv. 4-7) clearly depicts the image of the temple. In 1 Peter, a spiritual sacrifice will be offered in this spiritual house.

In 1 Corinthians, the major role of the Holy Spirit is related to the spiritual gifts that are used in the upbuilding of the church (1 Cor. 14). Thus the image of the church as the temple of the Holy Spirit correlates with the above findings as follows:

1. The temple is the dwelling place of God's powerful Spirit rather than simply a static building.
2. The church is in continuity and discontinuity with the congregation of the people of God in the Old Testament.
3. The oneness of the church is significantly emphasized.
4. The temple is depicted as a building in progress and the members as living stone, which indicates that the church is a movement and the members are the participants. The spiritual gifts of each individual are used to build up the church.
5. The lives of the members, not animals, are the sacrifice to be offered to God.

These corollaries are also related to the Wesleyan understanding of the church as discussed above.[89] As Asian Christians, however, we are facing challenges from all directions, including globalization, social and political oppression, religious pluralism, and the decline of our cultures that are threatened by modernization. To understand church as the temple of the Holy Spirit is to see our church as a church in the power of the Spirit rather than a church mainly associated with observance of rituals and devotion to a faith concerned with the salvation of individual souls.[90] The church under construction is not an empire; neither is it an institution nor an organization. The church is a community of worshiping people who are willing to offer the living sacrifice of our bodies and be empowered by the moving Spirit to overcome difficulties and hardship in following Jesus, and to participate in the struggle with the *minjung* to break the power and principalities of the world.

CONCLUSION

This study has identified an Old Testament origin for the images of "the *minjung*/people of God," "the congregation in the wilderness," and "the temple of the Holy Spirit." The images of "the community of disciples" and "the Word in flesh," on the other hand, are unique in the New Testament. In other words, the church in the New Testament is in continuity and discontinuity with the Israel of the Old Testament. While "the *minjung* of God" and "the congregation in the wilderness" emphasize the differentiation of God's people from other people in order to be in solidarity with the poor and the weak, the image of "Word in flesh" emphasizes the active participation of the church as the body of Christ in the world. The image of "the community of disciples" emphasizes a community with commitment and mission that is called and sent by Jesus, who was sent into the world by God. "The temple of the Holy Spirit" emphasizes the participation of each member in the process of the building up of the temple with their lives as the living sacrifice, empowered by the Spirit. The commonality of these five images is that the church is a group of people called to form a life-and-death community, which requires a movement rather than an organization or institution. This community's mission is to manifest the Word in proclamation and service-in-action, which is initiated and accompanied by the Holy Spirit toward the common goal set by God among the *minjung* in this world. The close relationship between the members of the church and the triune God is the basis of the community.

The Methodist movement was started as a reform movement inside the Church of England. It has parallels with the early Christian movement in Judaism. The danger of Christianity is that it loses its calling and mission given by God when it boasts its special status in relation to God.

In the Scriptures, in our Wesleyan tradition, and in the experiences of Asian Christians, the church is the church in mission (or in Outler's phrase: *a movement with a mission*),[91] which commits itself to the poor of the present age. From a scriptural perspective, this ecclesiology is fluid and multifaceted, for the church does not exist for itself but makes adaptations in different contexts to enhance its mission. How to keep the church as a dynamic missional church in our present age is our greatest challenge. So do Methodists have a doctrine of the church? If by a doctrine of the church, we mean a consistent and coherent but lively understanding of the church, then, yes, we do have one. But if we are looking for a static, fixed, and highly structured doctrine of the church, we would be better off if we did not have one.

CHAPTER FOUR

WORK ON EARTH AND REST IN HEAVEN: TOWARD A THEOLOGY OF VOCATION IN THE WRITINGS OF CHARLES WESLEY

Tim Macquiban

A great debt is owed to a host of scholars in the Charles Wesley tercentenary year, now past, for their contribution to scholarly editions of his writings and reflections on his life, literature, and legacy. Professors Newport and Campbell particularly are due thanks for their edition of papers on those themes. I offer here what can only at this stage be a work in progress on one aspect of a life much researched.

I heed Susan White's warning of the danger of trying to turn poetry into theology, for it is from Wesley's hymns and religious poetry that I shall derive much of what I want to say.[1] Yet the challenge for those of us in the Wesleyan traditions is to integrate Wesley's thought into our contemporary praxis, as we wrestle, Jacob-like, with Methodist theology. I am also aware that I may well not satisfy the purer historians by presenting ideas and concepts without a fuller understanding of the dates, context, and sources of Wesley's poetic imagination.[2] But I take inspiration from the work of people like Ted Runyon and ST Kimbrough, who have shown us how to appropriate for ourselves what Susan White calls the "hermeneutical imagination of Charles Wesley's work." Here the drama of Scripture coupled with the passionate experience of

Wesley for ministry and mission, the "wedding of faith and imagination through which a sense of the unknown comes" (Kimbrough), can illuminate and inform our experience of being part of a worldwide Methodist movement today. White concludes, "As the Church seeks to rekindle the religious imaginations of those who are mired in the prosaic and the mundane, those who look to Charles Wesley as a guide for their work will have much to contribute."[3]

Gareth Lloyd's recent work has highlighted how the legacy of Charles Wesley has been widely and diversely interpreted. From the beginning some have seen him as an "embarrassment to the Church that he helped to found,"[4] while others have made the case for this "paradoxical Anglican" forming not only something of Methodism's Janus-like identity but offering to the parent denomination the treasure of the hymns and at the same time a reminder of its continuing need for a second (or third?) reformation in the survival of a vigorous strand of reforming Anglicanism of which he was part.[5] Can Methodism today be seen as a product of the "compromise born of the different versions of John and Charles Wesley and of their followers"?[6] And if so, can we redeem Charles from the accusations that he turned his back on his primary vocation as an itinerant preacher, creating hostility and resentment among his fellow preachers? Can we see him as offering a wider vision of Christian vocation in a church that can no longer recognize the "ministry," that is, those ordained presbyters in connection, as univocal? To heed the challenges to British Methodism in recent decades, can we reclaim something from our Wesleyan heritage to substantiate the claim that *all* are called to minister "by virtue of their membership of the one body" (the church)? We might then be able to answer the criticism voiced by Shier-Jones (in her *Methodists Doing Theology*) that, while British Methodism boasts of its vocation and calling in the world, it "lacks the courage to believe in itself enough to define calling/vocation theologically or doctrinally."[7] So too in Larive's *After Sunday*, which points us to the way in which in many of our churches Christians have little sense of what in their weekday working world "constitutes a genuine Christian ministry."[8] This essay then explores what lessons we might draw from Charles Wesley's writings as we seek to understand what Paul Chilcote calls the "missional vocation" of Methodisms in the Wesleyan tradition and probe how "to serve the present age, my calling to fulfill" can be understood in terms of Wesley's theology of vocation.[9]

METHODOLOGY OF LEARNING FROM HYMNS

Franz Hildebrandt reminded us in the preface to the modern Wesley *Works* edition of the 1780 *Collection of Hymns:* "By their texts ye will know them." And we are grateful to him and Oliver Beckerlegge and others still working on those texts for making them available for present scholarship.[10] From the beginning scholars have recognized that in spirit, poetry and piety in hymns are closely connected as a "means of raising or quickening the spirit of devotion."[11] They are able to speak to us "transhistorically, transculturally, and transpersonally" in ways Geoffrey Wainwright (*Doxology*) and Frances Young (*Brokenness and Blessing*) have helped me and many others recognize that "the Spirit of Methodism is still most truly expressed in the best Wesleyan hymns which live on."[12] A biblical spirituality was at the center of the devotional life of Charles Wesley in that methodical pattern of holy living taught him by his mother of early rising, reading, and meditation, of writing and singing, to the praise and glory of God.[13] He wrote, "My every sacred moment spend / In publishing the Sinners' Friend."[14]

Here was a true "secretary of God's Praise" exercising, like his muse George Herbert, the sacred vocation of poet and pastor.[15] Francis Frost called it the "quasi-mystical expression of an intensely-lived personal faith."[16]

Hymns, especially when the "work of supreme devotional art by a religious genius,"[17] are perhaps more effective and more lasting than the sermons, despite the importance of the homiletical genre for Methodist doctrine. The hymns are "vehicles of doctrine and aids to devotion," forging the identity of the people called Methodists learning and singing.[18] They have a didactic as well as a doxological function, containing all things necessary to "instruct, to guide, and to envision the final hope of Christian existence" in the Methodist *ordo salutis*.[19] They are, or can be, tools for spiritual formation in the widest theological education program for our churches, as I have tried to demonstrate in "Our God Contracted to a Span."[20] Ted Campbell has reminded us of the importance of seeing Charles Wesley as *theologus*, using the hymns and poems as the means of grace through which may come a Wesleyan understanding of the "way of salvation." According to Langford, "To understand [his] theology, it is necessary to understand that it is theology-as-hymn."[21] It is characterized by realism. Charles's call, having heard the voice of God in his "conversion" of 1738, is to reform his inward dispositions in a way that then shapes his every action in responding by following Christ's way in outward works. This finds expression in the hymns and poems he offers by way of a guide for holy living and holy dying. They should therefore be seen as the product of his vocation as a minister, "as biblically based, experience-shaped theological expressions."[22]

Hymns are, however, not without their problems. Words are symbols, "gathering places of multi-layered meaning and means to participate in that meaning; . . . they are sacred," as Lathrop claims.[23] Texts can therefore be transformative. We understand ourselves and the world differently as a result of entering into the text. Imagination is crucial to the task of doing theology.[24] Hymns are to be regarded, as ST Kimbrough has argued, as icons of the Wesleyan tradition, multilayered vehicles of divine grace but not objects of special veneration—let the readers beware! The Wesleys were plagiarists extraordinaire, mercilessly plundering secular sources such as the classics and Milton; or rather, in kinder words, they were exponents of "inter-textuality," what Richard Watson calls "emotionally charged appropriation."[25] Such texts bring with them a "strong sense of multiple possibilities" by involving the reader in a dialogue that invites attentive reading and excites active perception leading to a response.[26] The question remains whether they can after three centuries continue to serve the present age in the way in which Bernard Manning observed they could in a flowery passage from *The Hymns of Wesley and Watts*. Hymns, he argued, brought the "glory of a mystic sunlight coming directly from another world. This transfigures history and experience. This puts past and present into the timeless Eternal Now."[27]

I want to argue, rather more prosaically, that in the same way that Wesley in his re-creative thought enabled Scripture to speak to our human condition in what it means to be a Christian, we can re-create a Wesleyan understanding of our calling, vocation, and work in the twenty-first century to serve the present age.

THE CONTEXT OF THE OXFORD INSTITUTES

Picking up the themes of the previous three Oxford Institutes (1992, 1997, 2002), I shall briefly look at "Good News for the Poor"; "Trinity, Community, and Power"; and "The New Creation." In 1992 we met in Oxford to consider what some have seen as the Wesleys' preferential option for the poor. Ted Jennings traced from his reading of the Wesleys' thought and praxis the "call and claim of justice for those who are vulnerable," as he later wrote.[28] ST Kimbrough introduced many of us to the *Hymns for the Poor* from the writings of Charles. He was to be remembered for the way in which he demonstrated to the church the need to accept its responsibility for the dispossessed of the earth. In summarizing the Institute's contributions, Douglas Meeks posed the question: "Can sanctifying grace create community in which the boundaries move according to the presence of Jesus Christ in the stranger, the radically other? Could such a community actually be an adumbration of the reign of God in which the poor actually and concretely hear good news?"[29]

Meeks elsewhere uses Wesley's model of life among and in service to the impoverished and disinherited to challenge contemporary understandings of stewardship in churches captive to the forces of modern market economics.[30] And in an article picking up from the theme of the 1997 Oxford Institute ("Trinity, Community, and Power"), Mary Elizabeth Moore highlighted the need to rediscover the wholeness of all ministry and the central significance of the *laos* from the Wesleyan ways of creating new structures for missional purposes in a covenantal community.[31] Randy Maddox reminded us of the need to maintain this trinitarian balance in a Wesleyan theology of responsible grace as we "proceed along the Way of Salvation," with the threefold structure of its theological framework: (1) the reverence for the God of holy love in God's prevenient grace, (2) the gratitude for the unmerited divine initiative in Christ in God's justifying grace, and (3) the responsiveness to the presence of the Holy Spirit in God's sanctifying grace.[32]

The Oxford Institute of 2002 looked at Wesleyan perspectives on the new creation (in which, incidentally, very little use was made of Charles Wesley). If God's shalom is to be realized, our work will focus on the need for a ministry of reconciliation (Moore) and the need to pay attention to "persons whom the world regarded as having no dignity" (Richey).[33] Ted Runyon pointed to "orthopathy" as a key Wesleyan note within the context of social holiness, a feeling of the needs of others in what Douglas Meeks reminds us is "not simply service of the poor but more importantly life with the poor."[34] And in this Wesleyan way of living, we cannot separate the place of worship from its relation to the mission of the church. As Dan Hardy reminds us, "God's interaction with the world was above all the gift of the new age, the new creation, the Kingdom of God," in a passionate expectation of the coming Lord.[35]

OUR CALLING: SOME DEFINITIONS

These themes from previous Oxford Institutes set the context for the discussion of our calling, our vocation, and our work.

First, the *call* is *God's call to holiness*, which is both a present reality in the process of Christian perfection and a future hope for pilgrims who are citizens of heaven, on the road, strengthened and enabled by the quickening power of God's spirit. For Charles Wesley, the pneumatological and eschatological dimensions of salvation's experience were important to his stress on heaven experienced here and now rather than confined to a future place beyond the skies. "Pardon and holiness and heaven" is a constant refrain of the hymns reflecting the threefold pattern of Wesleyan theology in "confirming faith, enlivening hope, kindling love,"[36] in Chilcote's words a "willingness to change, and expectation that God's grace is always available and a passion for God to show his love through our lives."[37]

As Charles in his expansion of the verse from Luke's Gospel (5:32), "I have come to call not the righteous," writes:

> Call (and give me ears to hear)
> My soul out of its fall,
> Call to godly grief and fear,
> To true repentance call,
> Call me Thine embrace to meet,
> To know and feel my sins forgiven
> Call me then to love complete,
> And call me up to heaven.[38]

For Wesley, the *perfection of holiness* is a relational concept, a matter of the heart in what Teresa Berger calls "the interiorization of soteriological reality in the heart of the believer."[39] At its center is the process of the restoration of the *imago Dei* in humanity. There is a passion for perfection in Wesley, who often pleads "restore us to our paradise" in conscious imitation of the Miltonic muse of *Paradise Lost.* In the quest for Christlikeness in our earthly lives, we are to be given a "new name," the name of Christ.[40] "This is our glorious calling's prize."[41] Methodist spirituality is infused with the duality of love of God and love of neighbor issuing in inward and outward holiness, of holiness of heart and life, framing the nature and practice of call and Christian vocation.[42] The participation in the divine life is made possible by the cosmic God become incarnate, who "deigns in flesh t'appear . . . and make us all divine, . . . made flesh for our sake that we might partake the nature divine."[43]

The *call*, then, is for individuals to repent and believe through inward holiness and for the people called Methodists to preach and witness and serve in outward and social holiness. It is a call for *all,* who are equal and known by name in the sight of God, whether Gentiles or Jews, rich or poor. For all are summoned to the gospel feast—a table that is open to all—neighbors and strangers alike. And all are called to return home as citizens of heaven even though displaced and alienated from the love of God by human sinfulness and ignorance. Berger calls this the "soteriological universalism" at the heart of Wesleyan theology in its hymns.[44] "For all my Lord was crucified, for all, for all my Savior died" and other hymns of universal redemption and God's everlasting love penned by Charles Wesley express the raison d'être of Methodist mission and the call to repentance. In the words of yet another hymn, the clarion call comes, "Arise, O God, maintain Thy cause! / . . . And *all* shall own Thou diedst for all."[45] The "feast of holy joy, and love" is prepared for all,[46] a feast of "never failing bread" provided by the all-gracious God,[47] who calls each one "by name / To the marriage of the Lamb."[48] So he bids, "Sinners, obey the gracious call / Unto the Lord your God return."[49]

And now we look at this call in terms of the *work* of God in creation and redemption and what that means for us human beings called to be coworkers with God. Miroslav Volf, in his *Work in the Spirit*, highlights the difficulties for us in a technological age reflecting on the thought processes of a preindustrial age in which work was often conceived of as toil and drudgery, slavery and a curse, concepts gleaned from a reading of post-fall biblical perspectives of humanity rather than as gainful and purposeful employment.[50] Esther Reed offers other more positive readings of biblical material.[51] Both want to root a contemporary understanding of work in the gifts or charisms that God has given to all people, which make for its honest and purposeful place in human well-being. The soteriological and eschatological dimensions of Moltmann's *Theology of Hope* connect work done under the inspiration of the Holy Spirit with the theme of the coming new creation.

The temptation is to see Charles Wesley as an unredeemed premodernist, whose worldview might be characterized by "work on earth, rest in heaven,"[52] but this characterization has to be seen in the context of his constant attacks on the often lazy, idle clergy and indolent workers of contemporary church and society. Brother John was not alone in his hostile attitude to those who used moments "triflingly." Charles's reading of the story of the laborers in the vineyard is an inspiration for his many reflections on this aspect of human activity.[53] For others, work is "wearisome pain" rather than "daily delight"[54] and a source of "worldly cares" that are dangers and snares for the spiritual life, not unlike the Wesleyan attitude to wealth. Labor is to be endured as long as life goes on, "the sweat of our brows, and the work of our hands"[55] as we "suffer on" until "our labor is complete."[56] We are to eat the "bread of care and sorrow."[57]

But from George Herbert ("Teach Me, My God and King") comes another strand, which Wesley takes up, seeing work in its entirety and its future sanctification, so that at the last, before the throne of God, we are judged by our earthly labors as much as by the inward disposition to God. The ultimate reward is heaven. In a reflection on the final discourses of Jesus with his disciples in John's Gospel (15:8), Wesley writes of his central view of work—that we work in order to praise God and to save souls by being an example and by ministering to the needs of the world. The faith evident through work well done, "faith working in love," is part of God's sanctifying work of grace through worship and service.

> One only work on earth I have,
> One only means Thy praise to show,
> My own and others' souls to save,
> Is all my business here below:
> I live Thy mercy's minister
> Myself to second life restored,
> A genuine child of God appear,
> A true disciple of my Lord.[58]

OUR CALLING TO FULFILL

I now turn to particular aspects of this call, giving attention to the christocentric nature of call that Wesley makes prominent through his use of the Scriptures. For Christ is the moral teacher who is the pattern for our lives and the yardstick of Christian ethics, in Luke Bretherton's term, the "ontological ground of morality."[59] To what extent is Christian vocation a "ministry of reconciliation, the call to invite all into a new community where justice is done and where freedom and love flourish"?[60] And how do the words of Charles Wesley match up to his and our praxis in allowing the religious thoughts to inform and shape the ministry and mission of the church?

First, it is a *call to serve* in every aspect of life, in a *ministry of purposeful work*.

The meanest labor is to be "hallowed" with a new direction as part of God's recreation. Some are given specific tasks and ministries in the life of the church, according to their God-given "talents, gifts and graces."

> My talents, gifts and graces, Lord,
> Into thy blessed hands receive;
> And let me live to preach thy word;
> And let me to thy glory live:
> My every sacred moment spend
> In publishing the Sinner's Friend.[61]

Charles's concern for all people, particularly the poor, was inherited from his father, Samuel. It was given a missional vocation as the mantle of George Whitefield was taken up in the fields of Kingswood and beyond in the post-Aldersgate realignment of the Wesleys' ministry.[62] As he wrote to Howell Harris the following year, 1740, "I now find a commission from God to invite all poor sinners, justified or unjustified, to his altar."[63] He shared this apostolic ministry to which he was called, albeit reluctantly, with preachers whose calling was equally recognized when their gifts and talents were confirmed. Such helpers had "nothing to do but to save souls . . . to spend and be spent" in this work. "And go always, not only to those that want you, but to those that want you most." They were chosen to be servants and not for privilege, giving themselves in a "revolutionary pattern of self-sacrificing love for the world."[64]

This did not come easily to Charles with his impatience at how others matched up to his standards, overreaching themselves with actions beyond their unordained status or underperforming in their path to perfection. He exercised his power over the assistants in the 1750s in a way that did not endear himself to them, particularly as he ceased to itinerate and was seen to be dependent on the efforts of his brother and fellow preachers to support his ministry. "Let there be no pretence to say that we grow rich by the gospel" were his brother's words that fell on less scrupulous ears.[65] John more directly warned Charles that his enemies "complain of your love for musick, company, fine people, great folks and the wane of your former zeal and frugality."[66]

Nevertheless, Charles continued to promote this serving, itinerating, tent-making ministry as one of apostolic zeal along the lines of the early church of the Acts of the Apostles:[67] "To turn thy kingdoms upside down / And set the world on fire."[68]

The "diverse gifts" given were to help the preachers fulfill their work and "never from their office move,"[69] those who were called to be a "shepherd of souls" and "faithful pastor" to the "little flock" who responded to the call of God.[70] The ministerial labors of such "messengers of heaven,"[71] as "fishers of men employ'd by Thee,"[72] as "steward[s] of His mysteries,"[73] were lifelong until the "evangelic toil" was done,[74] and they entered into the rest promised to those who endured to the end.[75] Wesley contrasted those unworthy ministers with those called and tried by "signs infallible."[76]

Their call was to go to the least and the lowest, as evidenced in hymns occasioned by visits to colliers in Newcastle[77] and Kingswood[78] as Wesley's hymns flowed from preaching and pastoral engagement in God's service to all. Such a service for the church below was a "constant heaven" in response to the "high commission" given to them.[79]

But this call to service was not confined to those called to be preachers. It was for all. Wesley wrote of the ministerial task for families, in holy households dedicated to useful, purposeful work in lifelong service and witness to God.

> Such our whole employment be,
> Works of faith and charity,
> Works of love on man bestow'd,
> Secret intercourse with God.[80]

And this call to service was a call *to be hospitable*, to offer hospitality to all, especially strangers, in a *ministry of just generosity*.

Just generosity and the practice of hospitality are means of holiness in answer to the call to discipleship of the Jesus who turns the world upside down, in radical discontinuity with the racial particularity of the Jews. Being good, pure, and holy, as Volf reminds us, "cannot be secured either by withdrawal or assimilation" in respect to the world in which we work.[81] Bretherton describes the way in which the giving and receiving of hospitality is an evangelical imperative.[82] To welcome the vulnerable stranger, to see her as representing Christ, and to give indiscriminately to the poor were key features of early Methodism in the eighteenth and early nineteenth centuries in England, which I have described at greater length in my doctoral thesis.[83]

Charles Wesley's giving to the poor is less well evidenced than his brother John's, but it is part of the "ascetical discipline undertaken primarily as part of their spiritual exercises" from the days of the Holy Club onward.[84] The poor and the strangers were "Jesus' bosom-friends," for whom Charles had a particularly tender spot. He justified it theologically from his understanding of the incarnate God, "humbled to the dust He is and in a manger lies," the Christ child in whom we see "the King of Glory, discern the Heavenly Stranger, so poor and mean, His Court an Inn, His cradle is a Manger."[85] The pity and awe excited by such debasement should stir the hearts of all the faithful in response to the needs of the poor. The imperative of words from Matthew 25:34-40 Wesley describes thus:

> Drink to a thirsty Christ I give,
> An hungry Christ I feed,
> The stranger to my house receive,
> Who here shall lay his head.[86]

Because we ourselves are strangers to God's grace through disobedience, we should seek God in the other, just as Ruth reminds us of all "strangers and foreigners," who are now God's "purchased people" despite being "forlorn, abandon'd and despised."[87] Whoever offers preachers and others "an hospitable welcome" "receives, not angels unawares, but Christ and God himself receives."[88] In encountering those who are "hospitably kind," the word is heard as God responds through the offer of love.[89]

Making room for the stranger, in a shared hospitality within community experienced more widely, is a faithful response to God's call. In this, the vocation of Christian life is "learned, lived, and sustained through holy friendship and faithful practices that open us to God's grace."[90] The gospel feast, so often taken by Wesley as the metaphor for the limitless nature of such grace, is the fullest expression of God's hospitality toward us to which we must respond.[91]

> Come, sinners, to the gospel feast;
> Let every soul be Jesu's guest;
> Ye need not one be left behind,
> For God has bidden all mankind.[92]

The call is to *follow Jesus Christ* and his example as Master, carpenter, Good Physician, friend of sinners, and pastor to all people in a *ministry of healing and reconciliation.*

From this notion of the virtue of hospitality comes the imperative to welcome and serve others following the example of Jesus' ministry, "because it is a holy and just thing to do."[93] Charles Wesley was clearly committed to a serving ministry following his Lord. The power and passion of his preaching were widely attested as John Williams of Kidderminster recorded on hearing him preach in the open air outside Bristol in 1740.[94] There were "evident signs of a most vehement desire . . . to convince his hearers . . . of the needed reconciliation to God." His moods swung from exhilaration to despair, from melancholy to compassion. He was intensely loyal yet had a quick and fiery temper which made him enemies as well as admirers.[95] His sympathy for the mourners and the oppressed was in line with the new benevolent spirit of the age: "I am peculiarly called to weep with you that weep . . . and those who suffer most find as near me as my own soul."[96]

Others did not always detect this sympathy in his brother John. Charles's hymns express this same evangelical concern for the poorest of the poor. For him, compassion was one of the supreme tests of whether a professing Christian really does have the Spirit of Jesus at work in her heart and life.[97] We have a picture of a devoted family man whose own sorrows and tragedies allowed him empathy with his audience. He was "singularly tender and affectionate in his manner when addressing those that were afflicted in mind, body, or estate."[98] He could be a reconciler of those at odds as well as the one who purged the preachers of those he felt needed to go in the turbulent decade after his marriage.[99] The assessment by Sally, his wife, is naturally sympathetic given their closeness. She wrote, "His most striking excellence was humility; . . . [he] disliked power, avoided pre-eminence and shrunk from praise."[100]

Several have pointed to Charles's physical ailments and illnesses as being at the root of his concern for wholeness of body as well as spirit. Was his retirement from the itinerant ministry after 1756 because of family commitments alone or because of the strain of conflict with his brother and other preachers resulting in illness?[101] His theology of suffering was perhaps a reflection of his struggles with physical pain, suffering, and melancholy resulting from the loss of family members, which made for an abundance of therapeutic imagery employed in his verse.[102] The death of self that came with the spiritual journey in an ascetic response was also the overcoming of the demands of the flesh in pursuit of the higher calling.

How else can we understand the extraordinary verses penned at the time of his wedding to Sally? These verses extolled the virtues of an anticipated "second Bridal-Day" when both would meet in heaven "within the Arms Divine," to which Sally penned in the margin—"Amen!"[103] In all things, Christ was the great exemplar. Discipleship meant that every believer was a "servant of His servant still, My Pattern I pursue,"[104] a pattern for compassionate service of fellow human beings, of honest work as the "son of the Carpenter," the "servant of all, to toil for man" in a life of sacrificial service; "And all I think, or speak, or do, / Is one great sacrifice."[105]

> Superfluous luxury they hate,
> Inured to toil they suffer on,
> On Jesus in His members wait,
> Their servants for His sake alone;
> And while they in His work abide,
> They trust their Master to provide.[106]

The call is therefore in part to suffer and bear burdens for the sake of Christ in a ministry of costly discipleship.

Charles's early ministry was marked by the persecution that he and John suffered at the hands of the mobs and with clerical taunts.

He was "a courageous and determined man" in the exercise of his ministry.[107] He declared that he would "preach the word in season and out of season tho' they [the bishops] and all men forbid me." "How can anyone," he wrote, "dare deny they [his lay helpers] are sent by God?"[108] Methodists were regarded as disturbers of the peace and wreckers of social harmony to be stopped by any means, fair or foul.[109] Even so, Charles lost the confidence of the preachers when he forsook the dangers of travel for the safety of city social life.

Nevertheless Charles's domestic sadness and external conflicts reinforced in him a theology of suffering as a consequence of his calling. He acquired a lively sense of all the distractions offered by the world, the flesh, and the devil even in domestic bliss.[110]

> Christ's afflictions now are mine,
> Now I answer God's design,
> For the Head and Body's sake,
> Jesus' cup and cross partake.[111]

Ministry is a sharing in the Gethsemane experience of Christ: "The cup from his Father receives, / That I my vocation may see."[112] It is a sharing also in the apostolic example of Paul and the early apostles. Like them, we are called to "labor hard . . . through grief and pain, / Through toils and deaths, we follow Thee,"[113] with the assurance of "my calling's heavenly prize" at the end in suffering for righteousness' sake and in daily dying so that the eternal crown may be claimed. Preachers are called to vindicate a suffering God by all they do, despite the "hellish hate" of those opposed to the gospel.[114]

The call is to witness to *unity in diversity* with a dynamic model of Trinity at the heart of a *ministry of unity*.

Charles's loyalty to the Church of England, particularly in the period after 1750 when the Methodists started to drift away from or be rejected by the mother church, has long been held against him. His obsessive and inviolable attachment to the church of his birth and upbringing has led some to ignore the vigorous critique he often made of its leadership and condition.[115] When Methodism reached the crossroads in 1784, his opposition to the ordinations and the setting up of parachurch institutions led him into increased estrangement from the Methodist movement. His burial in the churchyard of St. Marylebone Parish Church and not in his brother's chapel in City Road near his mother's resting place is indicative of this tension. For Charles, the Church of England was the "Old Ship," to be rescued and not abandoned to the rocks. He wrote to his brother John in 1755 that his fears about the preachers' growing strength meant that they should "insist on that natural affection for our desolate mother."[116]

Needless to say, the preachers did not see it his way and would have been happy to see her carted off to a retirement home! Charles continued to urge Methodists at Wednesbury and elsewhere in 1756 to continue in the "Old Ship": "let nothing hinder your going constantly to church and sacraments."[117] A loyal group of "Church" Methodists continued after his death until the sacramental controversy of the 1790s drove them into the wilderness.[118]

For Charles the unity of the church and its place in the wider Christian communion were important. Methodists were neither schismatics nor Dissenters against whom he penned critical and polemical verses in defense of unity. His sense of loyalty to his family—even when some drifted into Roman Catholicism—and his church brought a more catholic perspective that John's *Catholic Spirit* never quite realized. The unity of local fellowships should mirror the unity of the church itself; that was his "high calling's hope," that the church below would echo the unity of the church triumphant gathered to God. His hymn "The Communion of Saints" reflects this aspiration:

> Build us in one body up,
> Call'd in one high calling's hope;
> One the Spirit whom we claim;
> One the pure baptismal flame;
> One the faith, and common Lord;
> One the Father, lives, adored.[119]

The oneness of the church was naturally centered on Christ, who called all authentic Christians into a unity of fellowship, service, and worship, even though divided in the expression of doctrine and exercise of ministry. Friends were to be "gathered into one" in a supportive fellowship of pilgrims on the road, the path to perfection, together. "To our high calling's glorious hope, we hand in hand go on."

> Love, like death, hath all destroyed,
> Rendered our distinctions void!
> Names, and sects, and parties fall,
> Thou, O Christ, art all in all![120]

And so to the last aspect, which is to recognize that the call is to *worship as work* in a shared ministry with the *communion of saints*.

What we do here below in our worship is an activity done out of hope, which anticipates a world we hope for beyond present reality, an anticipatory and doxological function before "the final unqualified eschatological appearance of God's *doxa* . . . glory, at the end of time."[121] In our worship together, the social benefit of praising God is to connect us to the reality that is God in the supreme work of humanity. We are called to love and praise. The "chief end of man [*sic*] is to praise God and to enjoy him for ever," as the Westminster Confession reminds us. Christ is the *leitourgos* in whose place each of us as a worship leader stands in trepidation. Charles Wesley's role as the "sweet singer of Methodism" places him in a unique position, offering his hymns as tools for instruction and for formation as holy people. The hymns are "learning and holiness combined," leading us to yield to his guidance in training and fitting us "up for heaven," "for the sky."[122] Charles's hymns reflect the myriad responses to God's call, experienced in the different forms we have explored, graciously enabling each disciple to reaffirm her or his true vocation.[123] Worship then becomes for us the "vocation of a lifetime and a joyful obligation" that we need to take seriously, not just on Sundays but in our everyday lives. We offer our worship as a humble sacrifice, moments in our work as well as in our worship when God is revealed in the encounters with the Divine in our midst. We need to understand what Wolterstoff calls the "rhythmic alternation between work and worship, labor and liturgy," which is "one of the significant distinguishing features of a Christian's way of being-in-the-world."[124]

Charles does not then sideline worship as something peripheral to life but sees it as a central component of life dwelling within it.

> O God of our life, We hallow Thy name,
> Our business and strife is Thee to proclaim;
> Accept our thanksgiving for creating grace,
> The living, the living shall shew forth Thy praise.[125]

We are born to praise. God, who "callest babes to sing Thy praise and manifest Thy power," uses the hymns of Charles not merely to teach us holiness and the doctrine of Christian perfection, but to celebrate the experience of salvation in the struggle for and anticipation of the coming of Christian perfection.[126]

CHARLES WESLEY'S IMAGES AND METAPHORS OF LIMINALITY

To take us over that threshold to reach our "holy calling's prize" and "make us all divine" as we claim "Thine image in Thy Son,"[127] the same image that we call upon God to "stamp . . . on [our] heart[s],"[128] Charles uses a range of images and metaphors that help us cross the boundaries between us. Bretherton uses the Barthian motif of near and distant neighbors to make the distinction between the community and the church, a series of frontiers that are constantly changing.[129]

Though "now we lie in *deepest night*," we "soon shall see the gospel day emerging into *glorious light*."[130] "Christ whose glory fills the skies" uses the Miltonic images of the blinded Samson imprisoned in the dungeon of self and released to a glorious freedom, echoing the hymns' frequent use of the image of imprisonment and release, a theme I have explored at greater length elsewhere.[131]

Both Wesleys used the spatial images of *porch* and *door* in their theological framework for the story of salvation. The "door to the penitent poor" is opened that all may come in, "rescued from sin."[132] The prison doors are opened to all who "obey the heavenly call."[133] A mark of the authenticity of Christian hospitality is what we do for those unjustly imprisoned in all manner of situations.

We are all *strangers* and *pilgrims* in search of our ultimate *rest* and *home*. "How happy is the pilgrim's lot!" writes Wesley, celebrating our lack of possessions that last and our aspiration to reach that "country in the skies."[134] In moments of pessimism at the earthly burdens we bear, he reminds us that each is but "a poor sojourner below," "going where they all have gone"; "let me my last stage pass o'er, die, to appear on earth no more."[135] Like Adam and Eve, coming out of Eden, we pass on "hand in hand," called to "our glorious hope" in an earthly pilgrimage through a "vale of woe" until the paradise lost is regained.[136]

The *dispossessed* are promised *Canaan* and a land of milk and honey as metaphors for this bliss beyond, a mountain on which Isaiah's vision of "a table for the world His guest" is spread out, prefiguring the "gospel feast" that Christ inaugurates.[137]

For those with nothing in their hands, *naked* and *poor*, they shall be "clothed with Thy holiness"[138] and given the "*crown* of perfect love"[139] at the end of their procession along the "consecrated way"[140] brought to a place where a "brighter crown" awaits[141] as they "rise to the *prize* of our glorious calling,"[142] their "patient faith" is crowned and they "enter into rest, and then on Thy perfection feast" (emphasis added).[143]

BIBLICAL NARRATIVE THEOLOGY

Charles Wesley uses biblical language as if it were his mother tongue, almost unaware he is doing it, and according to Berger, he "moves within the biblical world, its pictures, vocabulary, and imagery" like mosaics of scriptural texts.[144] But they are far more than this as he stretches out meanings beyond the context, which allows the imagination of readers to range far and wide, taking them into his experience of the story of salvation and challenging them to appropriate it for themselves.

In retelling the story of the Methodists, Wesley skips into the language of the story of God's salvation of the particular people of Israel. Moses and the people of Israel are paradigmatic in the story of God's providence as we pass through the wilderness to the promised land.

Captain of Israel's host, and guide
Of all who seek the land above,
Beneath thy shadow we abide,
The cloud of thy protecting love:
Our strength thy grace, our rule thy Word,
Our end, the glory of the Lord.

By thy unerring Spirit led,
We shall not in the desert stray;
We shall not full direction need,
Or miss our providential way;
As far from danger as from fear,
While love, almighty love, is near.[145]

So too with the story of "Wrestling Jacob." We are placed in the story as Israel emerges from the wilderness to be given a new name, a changed identity, and a world to be won for God, whose name is "pure universal Love."[146]

The approach of a gracious God to a people afar is explored in the great narrative poem of the "Good Samaritan."[147] Here is a God who reaches out like the generous father to the prodigal son.

To every one whom God shall call
The promise is securely made;
To you far off, he calls you all,
Believe the word which Christ hath said.

Here is a deep-felt compassion as one "is moved as to one's bowels" (Greek *splagchnizoma*), feeling the pain of another as if it were one's own.[148]

In the presentation of the story of Martha and Mary, Wesley makes it clear that both "secular and sacred care" are sanctified by God.[149] In the hymn "For a Believer, in Worldly Business," we are urged to "choose the better part: serve with careful Martha's hands and humble Mary's heart." For "every work I do below, I do it to the Lord." But with the adoration of Mary such worldly business is elevated in praise of God.[150] The capacity for work to "dry up my heart" is recognized. But essentially "work for Thy great praise design'd" can be purified in obedience to God's will.[151]

In the postresurrection account of the encounter of Mary Magdalene with the risen Lord, we are presented with a paradigm of the post-Aldersgate awakened soul. First "Jesus calls her by her name," and she "hears the voice Divine." She responds with obedience to "spread the gospel-word" and to "testify all the wonders of Thy grace" so that all may know that "Christ hath died, and rose for all." Encapsulated within seven verses is the entire salvific nature of Christian calling and vocation.[152]

CONCLUSION

Essentially for Wesley, the call is for *now* and for *everyone*. "This is the time, no more delay,"[153] "he calls you now,"[154] a *kairos* moment for each to respond to the call to join the gospel feast prepared for all. It is a moment of transformation; "Me for Thine own this moment take, / And change, and thoroughly purify: / Thine only may I live, and die."[155]

The true vocation of the Christian is centered on love, on being conformed to the image of a loving God and having the mind of Christ, the loving Savior. The mind of Christ, filled with the pure, universal love of God for all, is manifest in us when we do what Christ did, expressed in works of piety, and walk as Christ walked, expressed in works of mercy.[156] The servanthood of those so called is evident only if both are present.

> Thy every perfect servant, Lord,
> Shall as his patient Master be,
> To all Thine inward life restored,
> And outwardly conformed in Thee.[157]

Yet the tension between aspects of such a calling remains.

> What is our calling's glorious hope
> But inward holiness?
> For this to Jesus I look up
> I calmly wait for this.[158]

However, this call is not in the quietism of Moravian stillness. Rather, it is to be found in the Wesleyan social activism embedded in the lives of women like Mrs. Naylor, "a nursing mother to the poor," to whom "her life, her all bestow'd," whose example Wesley heralds in death as one in whom "doing good" was her "whole delight."[159] Here was faith evident in good works, with Methodists "laboring to do all things well."[160] For without such works, "faith . . . is not the true, the living principle of grace," which "when all its toils are past" gains "the promise of pure love at last."[161]

Nevertheless within the writing and experience of Charles Wesley there is a tension between this ascetic spirituality driven by his desire for him and all Methodists to press toward perfection as a goal of Christian living and the more mystical spirituality that could have him plunge into the oceans of God's love in an instantaneous experience of the kenotic God who bids us leave self behind: "Now let me gain perfection's height; / Now let me into nothing fall."

This suggests a spirituality divorced from or above the ordinary stuff of life and labor.[162] Martin Groves helpfully explores this bipolarity, this problem of connecting the enraptured spirituality of his inner life with the busyness of the preacher and family man, in which he suggests a disjunction between inward and outward religion.[163] Or is there a more holistic spirituality, a dynamic interaction of such works of piety and works of mercy as Chilcote suggests in which spirituality and morality are brought closer together?[164]

Consider this powerful epitaph of Charles Wesley:

As a Christian Poet He Stood Unrivaled;
And his hymns will convey instruction and consolation
To the faithful in Christ Jesus,
As long as the English language shall be understood.[165]

His hymns still have the power to move and transform lives. Raymond George wrote that "Wesley hymns and the Methodist way of using hymns in general are one of the greatest treasures which they can contribute to the Universal Church."[166] But it is a treasure that needs careful handling and proper exposition. We "need to help the Church be aware of the distinctive and precious heritage of hymnic art which it possesses."[167]

The challenge for us, teachers and practitioners of Arminian Wesleyan spirituality, is to translate this and other scholarly papers into formational tools for world Methodism in its different forms in the twenty-first century as we seek to revitalize the missional vocation of the people called Methodists. The hymns of Charles Wesley are the inspiration behind this difficult but worthwhile task of bringing together faith and works in a renewed and transformational synthesis that is "at the heart of the proclamation of the Gospel."[168] That is the basis of our calling. We are raised up for evangelism and mission but must not be deluded into thinking that it means only ministering to the needs of those who are our immediate neighbors. Rather, our true vocation, as Bonhoeffer reminds us, is to live respon-sibly by taking up a position against the world in the world.[169] It requires a *radical hospitality*, which transposes boundaries, to serve others and welcome them, "to readjust our identities to make space for them."[170] It calls us to a ministry of *healing and reconciliation* in a divided world. For, as Greg Jones reminds us, "hospitality and forgiveness are two central formative and imaginative treasures of our faith."[171] It will mean that "the vocation of the church is to sustain many vocations," allowing a variety of vocations to develop and flourish within our churches.[172]

Charles Wesley's preaching and poetry were powerful tools for transformation for which, in his tercentenary year and beyond, we give thanks to God. From his poetic imagination, informed and shaped by biblical narratives given a new power in the light of his grace-filled experience, we derive texts and meanings that help forge our Methodist identity through our greater understanding of our calling. These become then for us subversive acts of profound hope in a fractured world, making sense of who we are and how we act in this Wesleyan tradition, connecting heart and mind, worship and work.

I conclude with some words of a modern-day Wesley, the British Methodist hymn writer Fred Pratt Green, whose work deals with these themes for our present age and inspires the next generation to take up the pen and communicate them afresh in the Wesleyan spirit. Green's hymn, "The Church of Christ in Every Age," suggests that our mission, in obedience to Christ, is:

> To care for all, without reserve,
> And spread his liberating Word.[173]

CHAPTER FIVE

"To Serve the Present Age, Our Calling to Fulfill": A Different Church for a Different World

Ivan Abrahams

Power in itself is not evil. It is the gift of God given to every person and every society. The corruption of power through the selfishness of man, resulting in the deprivation of power from his fellowman, is evil. Churches and church members denying their participation in power structures are prone to become instruments of oppression by over-looking the magnitude and depth of the sinful selfishness of man which seeks to entrench itself in the structures of society.[1]

The people of all the nations will be gathered before him. Then he will divide them into two groups. . . . [He will say to the righteous people,] . . . "Come and possess the kingdom which has been pre-pared for you. . . . I was hungry and you fed me, thirsty and you gave me a drink; I was a stranger and you received me in your homes, naked and you clothed me; I was sick and you took care of me, in prison and you visited me." (Matthew 25:32-40 TEV)[2]

I write as an African and a Christian of Methodist heritage who hails from South Africa. I am adamant that I shall win a space for Africa's contemporary plight, not as a beggar or an apologetic, but as one who has proudly sought to remain true to a Wesleyan heritage and faithful to a theology that calls us to spread scriptural holiness throughout the land by the proclamation of the evangelical faith. Yet as I survey the experiences of poverty, pain, and disease of my country and the continent of Africa, I admit to the need for transformation of our polity and practices both as church and as citizens of the world in which we live. Ironically, the social, religious, and political institutions that silenced my ancestors are now calling on me to reflect on service and vocation.

The theme of the twelfth Oxford Institute constrains me to draw on the values, principles, and vision of a different world—one cruelly denied and removed from my forebears—in essence, a world in which their humanity cried out for affirmation. Yet this moment awakens within me the need to celebrate my heritage, partially as a descendant of a resilient slave-settler community and partially as one with a mixture of blood from the near-extinct Khoi and San— blood that continues to course through my veins. I speak as one brought up on the Cape Flats of Cape Town, having lived and grown up in the shadow of Table Mountain. The Flats is not the privileged part of Cape Town but a territory of deep inequity of land and resource distribution. Cape Town—that tip of Africa still today referred to by Nguni speakers as Koloni, the colony. The legacy of British imperialism and colonial domination is still hard to shake off in contemporary indigenous language and even democratic South Africa.

Ironically, Britain commemorated two hundred years of the abolition of the transatlantic slave trade in March 2007. Herbert McGonigle[3] argues that this anniversary should have a special significance for the Wesleyan Holiness people around the world as "the father of the Holiness movement," John Wesley, was one of the dominant voices against slave trafficking and certainly upheld the work and motivation of the abolitionist William Wilberforce. Just as many scholars, economists, and leaders of civil society unambiguously argue that global economy and neoliberalism fuel a different form of slavery, so too would it be necessary to unpack and analyze words and phrases such as "serve the present age" and "fulfillment of one's vocation" in our context of a "global village."

After roughly two-and-a-half centuries of economic growth following the main thinkers of the Enlightenment who believed in the essential equality of humanity and the ability of societies in all parts of the world to share in economic prosperity, I believe that God's future lies in a different world: a world in which all can begin to flourish through respect and dignity, irrespective of race, culture, gender, language, or sexual orientation. The burning question that remains unanswered, however, is, How do we "serve the present age" and fulfill our vocations when the outcomes of economic globalization and neoliberalism are being defined by an ever-increasing gap between rich and poor, the ongoing impoverishment of Africa, and the resultant degradation of our biosphere? How do we exercise leadership from church and society when the edifices of power within the International Financial Institutions (IFIs), such as the International Monetary Fund (IMF), World Bank, and World Trade Organization (WTO), impose policies and prescriptions that negate Africa's democratic sovereignty? I want to believe that the "present age" is bound up with God's future and that our salvation—similarly linked—lies in our vocational and mission choices that promote mutual coexistence, the flourishing of humanity and healing for God's world. The eschatological question then, is, How will we be true—even unconsciously so—to the vision of a different world portrayed in Matthew 25, where God is the center of our attention in work and ministry to the marginalized, impoverished, alienated, and diseased of our nations and world?

Charles Villa-Vicencio, a Methodist theologian, pointed out during a time of apartheid-entrenched national security that Wesley's doctrine of perfect sanctification holds the key to a broader Wesleyan perspective, an acknowledgment that God's activity of social transformation includes human participation. The ultimate meaning of sanctification, said Villa-Vicencio, is to "pursue this broad theological horizon . . . [that] could assist us to become co-creators and active partners with God transforming South Africa."[4] Such was the vision of the service and vocation of a "different church for a different world" then; and I believe it holds good for us now. Therefore, just as Pliny the Elder believed that Africa always offers something new, I offer this exploration of service and vocation for a different church in a different world as the vocation for justice, peace, and human equity—some virtues the current architecture of world power appears to be unwilling to consider or incapable of delivering. But it is to that transformed age—the age of God's future already present in our midst in the lives and experiences of the poor, marginalized, and dehumanized—that this present age needs seriously to focus its mission and vocation. For God is to be found nowhere else.

THE HISTORICAL LEGACY OF AN ENSLAVED CONTINENT

In the same way that South Africa's apartheid framework spawned systems of "separate development," privileging one group over another, premised on the lie that separate development and developmental equity were the same, so it appears that global capital has privileged, and continues to privilege, the West and its allies against Africa and the rest of the two-thirds world. I am of the firm conviction, therefore, that similar dynamics and much more are at work in an age that I have no hesitation in labeling "global economic apartheid."[5] The extent of this apartheid is, however, far more devastating, and you will hear me describe how nations and continents, and especially Africa, have fallen and continue to fall into slavery as a result of the current global economic system and its rules that extract—and have extracted for hundreds of years—more than they plow back.

Despite the political victory of Wilberforce and the antislavery act, descendants of enslaved forebears in the two-thirds world still experience unparalleled systems of control, domination, and disempowerment by the wealthier nations. For this reason it is safe to say that slavery has mutated into a multiplicity of structures that fetter people and keep nations in bondage today. While two hundred years ago its form was the inhuman, brutal, and forced removal of people from their lands of birth, its form in the twenty-first century targets those same continents in order to maintain political and economic dominance. The structures that disguise contemporary slavery may appear successful, but they continue to discriminate. Joerg Rieger puts it succinctly when he argues that despite the challenge for Methodism to remain "relevant and centered" in the twenty-first century, we are sucked into the powers that be, which are now defined by global capitalism—an economic system that marginalizes large parts of the population and where inequality is becoming more severe. We witness a new system of slavery that is more heinous and cruel than what Wesley could have imagined—more cruel than the European and American slave trades ever were, since people are becoming more and more commodified.[6]

The question arises, *How did this happen?* The answer is that slavery has mutated over the past five centuries, and what we call economic globalization today is the contemporary version of slavery.[7] But while slavery of two hundred years ago reduced humanity to a tradable commodity on the global market because of a black skin, contemporary global economic expansion makes every human being expendable, and therefore, the continent of Africa becomes the most vulnerable and expendable, especially when the economy assumes a divine rationale. Patrick Bond says—and I agree with him—that Africa is to a large extent a centuries-old "looted continent." In a contemporary affirmation of Walter Rodney's analysis of the underdevelopment of Africa by Europe, Bond recognizes the colonial advantage of trade by force, deception, rape, theft, and pillage that define the Western world's patterns of political and economic relations with Africa. Bond says,

Africa is a continent looted through slavery that uprooted and dispossessed around 12 million Africans; land grabs; vicious taxation schemes; the nineteenth-century emergence of racist ideologies to justify colonialism; the 1884–85 carve-up of Africa in a Berlin negotiating room, into dysfunctional territories; the construction of settler-colonial and extractive-colonial systems—of which the apartheid, the German occupation of Namibia, the Portuguese colonies and King Leopold's Belgian Congo, were perhaps only the most blatant—often based upon tearing black migrant workers from rural areas (leaving women with vastly increased responsibilities as a consequence); Cold War battlegrounds—proxies for US/USSR conflicts—filled with millions of corpses; other wars catalysed by mineral searches and offshoot violence such as witnessed in blood diamonds and coltan; societies used as guinea pigs in the latest corporate pharmaceutical test . . . and the list continues.[8]

To illustrate my point on turning an African country into a "slave economy," I turn to a newly defined democracy such as the Democratic Republic of Congo (DRC), which has sought close ties and guidance from South Africa in (re)building its democracy. On June 29, 2007, the DRC put together its first national budget and announced a total budget expenditure framework of about $2.4 billion. This amount is equivalent to the sum spent by the United States in less than two weeks for the occupation of Iraq. How, under conditions devastated by two wars in which 3.5 million people died, can a nation rebuild itself with this kind of budget? By comparison, France, which, like the DRC, has a population of around 60 million, has a budget of $520 billion, in other words more than two hundred times the Congolese budget. The subsoil of DRC is referred to as a "geological scandal"—a treasure of mineral resources—and the country's agricultural land is incredibly fertile, but the IMF believes that this is an appropriate budget, especially as its officials await debt repayment slightly in excess of 50 percent of that budget. We await DRC parliamentary reactions and the reactions of civil society to the IMF's subversion of democracy by riding roughshod over any people's participatory process ushered in by democratic elections.[9]

It is important to acknowledge that although the slave trade was abolished in England by an act of Parliament two hundred years ago, human bondage and social and economic injustice still remain a major issue. Slavery and its legacies have been critical in shaping the cultural history of the modern world. We cannot escape the fact that much of Britain's wealth—many cities filled with cathedrals, palaces, and corporate houses—is built on an unjust system that extracted millions of Africans from their homeland as chattel to supply the slave labor market. Much of what is seen in England is the result of the slave trade and slave-based industries that supplied raw materials from the colonies to sustain the British Empire. As Wilf Wilde says in his commentary on Mark's Gospel, "Before we can Make Poverty History, we need to understand rather more of the history of how poverty has been made."[10] How is it that a biblical commentary, which is at the same time a political and historical commentary, becomes a necessary contribution to Christian social thought and practice? The issue is that British, American, and European versions of colonialism require a modicum of honesty in understanding how they allowed Africa to remain underdeveloped and continue to do so in different ways today. It is, as Wilde insists, a matter of an honest and faithful telling and retelling of your history to your children and children's children of how your ancestors benefited from the wealth, labor, and resources of my immediate and past ancestors. The legacy of an enslaved continent is ongoing enslavement and Western economic ascendancy through international financial institutions.

GLOBALIZATION, ECONOMIC GLOBALIZATION, AND THEIR DISCONTENTS

Globalization is generally accepted as an ongoing process of human, political, and international development. On the whole its effects, as they may relate to technological and scientific advances, are relatively benign and often beneficial with regard to social and political relationships. Economic globalization, on the other hand, is driven by a conglomeration of powerful nations, multinational corporations, the World Bank, the International Monetary Fund, and the World Trade Organization. This system, says Rogate Mshana, program executive of the World Council of Churches, has

widened the gap between the rich and the poor and has increased absolute poverty in the world (3 billion people living on less than two dollars a day and 1.2 billion on less than one dollar a day). Inequality is vivid, with 5% of the richest earning 144 times more than the poorest 5%. Twenty per cent of the world population owns 80% of the global wealth. In Africa, 65% of the inhabitants live on less than one dollar a day and as many as 87% on less than two dollars a day. . . . The environment is being mutilated and the earth is groaning. . . . The top 20% of the global rich is responsible for 53% of global pollution. . . . UNDP warns that this will affect the implementation of the Millennium Development Goals (MDGs) because poverty will not be halved in 2015, but 2147.

Mshana adds, "In the context of Africa, primary education will be delivered, not in 2015, but in 2130. That is 115 years late. . . . The elimination of avoidable infant deaths, not in 2015, but in 2165. That is 150 years late."[11]

Carmencita Karagdag, however, does not distinguish between globalization and economic globalization because, for her, the economies, ecologies, and life-support systems of the South, including Africa, have suffered "massive ruin."[12] Globalization, understood as a political project based on neoliberal ideology in order to keep the South in bondage to the North, is not value free. Of deeper concern, however, is the symbiotic link drawn by Karagdag between "globalization, the abuse of human rights through militarization—especially in Iraq—and the global ideological and faith relationships that cement partnerships in sustaining empire."[13]

The issue is not the claim that global capitalism has become the most successful economy to deal with human development in the world. There is a grain of truth in such a claim, but economic globalization is problematic for the manner in which it distances the wealthy from the poor and concentrates wealth in the hands of a few while impoverishing many and rendering many more redundant, unemployed, or unemployable.[14] A more disconcerting problem posed by global capital expansion is its all-pervasive, religious-like, "dogma" of principles often referred to as "economic fundamentals," such as "belt tightening" or "structural adjustment programs."[15] I reject out of hand this confusion of religious morality with neoliberal economics and give it attention later in this essay. The truth is that these mantralike assertions have caused confusion and promoted economic and political advantage for the wealthy nations. In so doing, global economics has become the invisible pillar of contemporary slavery.

TOWARD ECONOMIC AND GLOBAL JUSTICE

Ulrich Duchrow has warned us for some time now that the projected outcomes of a global, neoliberal capitalist economy are loss of life support for future generations and death if there is no U-turn immediately or in the short-term future.[16] Clearly the challenge that poorer nations face is not "starting the engine of the economy and approaching take-off for economic growth." If it were that simple, the African economies would have been soaring by now. Since global economic systems are human by design, they can be, need to be, and should be challenged and corrected for deficiencies. The deficiency of this death-inducing economy[17]—both realized and to be realized if it continues unfettered—is sufficient to take up a *kairos* challenge to our faith.

In the article "Political and Economic Wellbeing and Justice: A Global View,"[18] Duchrow raises the importance of "demythologising economics" by arguing that capitalism has to a great extent influenced people and interest groups by using the complexity of economics as an ideological "veil." In the midst of the triumph of capital and the collapse of Marxist-socialism in the 1980s, Duchrow grappled with biblical models such as God's option for the Hebrew slaves in Egypt, poverty and wealth in the modern era, and the use of countervailing force against capital. For Duchrow, the ecumenical concept of "responsible society" was inadequate to deal with the ascendancy of capital. Justice, for him, as for Mr. Wesley, consists of using church communities for economic alternatives such as projects that lend money without charging interest for profit; promoting production cooperatives on church-owned land; forming networks with countervailing forces; creating pressure from below to raise alternatives for the provision of basic needs; enabling people's participation in economic decisions; and holding in view the rights and needs of future generations.

We now turn to the African concepts of justice that complement our search for economic justice, signs for a different church and a different world.

UBUNTU/BOTHO IN ECONOMIC JUSTICE: ECONOMICS WITH A HUMAN FACE

Insofar as the neoliberal economic framework uses market mechanisms to apportion value to the resources and goods that enable life, says Puleng LenkaBula,[19] theological scholar and recently appointed vice president of the South African Council of Churches, it unwittingly perpetuates the hegemony of the market over and above other life-giving principles and values such as Botho/Ubuntu justice. *Botho* is a Sesotho word that encompasses personhood and humaneness, which roughly translated means that "a person is a person because of other persons."

According to LenkaBula's study, four elements of Botho/Ubuntu are of importance in its link with the economy. First, humaneness is about relationships and cooperation. A human being is shaped by cultural, genetic, historical, biological, and social relationships, not mechanical ones that may allow for competitiveness and individualism. Second, it is about respect and empathy for others and indicates a worldview that is sensitive to the ecosystem and leads to a communal responsibility for the sustenance of life. Third, it is about the deep interconnectedness of life and nurture of earth as a value that links to justice and fairness in the use of resources. Fourth, it links justice and economy, best described by the idiom: "all members of the family share the head of a locust."[20] This Setswana proverb indicates that in a precarious economy—as in times of drought—the African does not have to wait for abundance but understands that however little there is, it is worth sharing. The study highlights that sharing should not be limited to individuals, but it should extend to public and private management of national resources. The study further states that this concept is also a warning to governments set on neoliberal and capitalist monetary and fiscal policies.

WESLEY'S "EVANGELICAL ECONOMICS" AS ALTERNATIVE TO ECONOMIC GLOBALIZATION

In the biblical and Wesleyan sense, I am arguing that the only forms of justice that Wesleyans ought to recognize are God's justice and justice for the poor. Wesley's concern for people on the margins of society, the poor, the sick, and the imprisoned as well as his commitment to "a journey downward" to create a new world *with* the poor, on *their* terms and in *their* places, is well documented.[21] He undertook, for instance, to distribute a considerable amount of his income to the poor and to practice what he called "begging for the poor," whereby he solicited from the prosperous what the poor needed. Wesley had a "holistic concern for the wellbeing of all God's creatures' mind body and soul"; that was the reason for his medical clinics, meals for the poor, interest-free loans, orphanages, and schools.[22]

Theodore Jennings indicates that Wesley's evangelical economics addresses four main issues: the demystification of wealth, a preferential option for the poor, a protest against injustice, and stewardship as the redistribution of wealth.[23] Suffice it to say, however, that Wesley lived what he professed: that the gospel of Christ knows no religion but social religion; no holiness but social holiness. Some may say this is overplayed, but to distill the Wesleyan option for the poor in an "evangelical economics," let us examine Wesley's sermon "The Use of Money," frequently dismissed as an apology for primitive capitalism. Randy Maddox assists us here admirably in reminding us that the injunction to "gain all you can" merely stated the assumption that one should enjoy social responsibility in the manner one acquires property, capital, or the means of production. The injunction to "save" relates to an approach to self-denial in the use of resources that doesn't lead to waste and the indulgence of luxury. The command to "give" renounces the accumulation of anything beyond one's basic needs and advises the redirection of surplus possession to meet the needs of one's neighbor in want.[24] This understanding of stewardship is contrary to the economics of accumulation and greed. It is the heart of Wesley's evangelical economics. For him the criterion for every action was "how it was going to benefit the poor." For this reason he contended that visiting the poor was a means of grace alongside offering public prayer and partaking of the sacraments.

Wesley's economic ethic was more than an ethic of decision or personal choice. The Wesleyan tradition of practical living, homiletics, and theological treatise portrays a model of "holiness of heart and life" that, as early as the age of Enlightenment, refuses to separate the realms of life into secular and sacred or into the public and the private. Peter Storey makes the point that "John Wesley made the revolutionary discovery that you could not really be a Christian unless you engage with the poor of the earth" and further defines a Wesleyan Christian as "one who has made an intentional option to stand with the poor and marginalized of society, against the principalities and powers that hold all such in bondage."[25]

So far, so good, but how do we explain the earlier Methodist leadership of the 1960s and 1970s and—certainly until the late 1990s in South Africa and Africa—failing to come to grips with the nexus between faith and politics and faith and economics? I am not suggesting that we take a reconstructed eighteenth-century theological treatise and develop a twenty-first-century reaction to the global economic malaise. What I am suggesting is that we recognize that the poor are caught in a trap of death and despair orchestrated by people who are supposed to be regulating global economics—a life-and-death matter.[26] Their very dignity is being impaired by economic globalization that marginalizes and excludes them. In the same way that theology undergirded the slave trade in the eighteenth and nineteenth centuries, so also much of our current theology by omission or commission must plead guilty to collusion with the purveyors of global capital.

For this reason it is salient to turn to Wesley's General Rules, written in 1734, in which he prohibited "the buying and selling of the bodies and souls of men, women, and children, with the intent to enslave them." In "Thoughts upon Slavery"[27] published in 1774, he attacked the institution of slavery by affirming the dignity and human rights of Africans. Besides appealing to the Christian conscience of those involved in the slave trade, he cited human decency, natural law, and justice as reasons enough to abolish slavery. For Wesley, true Christianity was characterized by love of God and neighbor, and for this reason slavery was inhuman and unjust.

A further, telling point, seldom expressed in Wesleyan theology, is the power of the story of an African person's struggles for freedom and dignity. A specific example is "The Interesting Narrative of the Life of Olaudah Equiano," which confirms the doctrine of Christian perfection, especially the overlap of "works of mercy" and "works of piety," vibrantly alive in the last days of Wesley's personal life. It is this identification with the struggles of the marginalized, this solidarity with a slave's quest for human freedom, that motivates his writing, six days before his death on March 2, 1792, to encourage William Wilberforce to press on, in his crusade to abolish slavery within the British Empire and America.[28]

The injunction "to serve the present age, our calling to fulfill," in the face of global capital expansionism and debt is one of the biggest challenges this century faces. We are reminded that it is only as we hear the cries of the vast majority of debt-ridden, impoverished humanity and act in solidarity with them, especially in our understanding of the means of grace, that we have a chance to eradicate poverty and overcome its attendant forms of neocolonial slavery. John Wesley radically influenced theology and ethics more than two hundred years ago. Can his theologians, preachers, and people, two centuries later, do the same in the face of global capital expansionism and its "doctrines" of neoliberalism?

TOWARD AN AFRICAN AND WESLEYAN THEOLOGY OF GOD'S ECONOMY FOR LIFE AND FOR THE FUTURE

Methodism in South Africa, from an organized and institutional perspective, has frequently wrestled with its heritage in contexts of apartheid and more recently in a post-apartheid democratic South Africa.[29] Itumeleng Mosala, a Methodist and black liberation theologian, reflecting on Methodism in the context of an apartheid state of emergency, suggests that Wesleyan theology—if it stands for social emancipation—will need to make its location amidst the poor, vulnerable, and marginalized in South Africa a theological priority. He therefore called for a dynamic revision of the doctrine of Christian perfection by challenging Methodism to "take seriously the discourses of the struggle of oppressed people."[30] I suggest that this challenge remains relevant today within the context of global capital expansion and its resultant slavery on the African continent and elsewhere. Our vocation to "serve the present age" therefore challenges us to understand the heart of the doctrine of sanctification—Wesley's standard of excellence, Christian perfection—by which the gift of grace in Christian life is to be measured through the voices, stories, and characters on the African continent that seek to redress such imbalances of wealth and power distribution.

I now offer three African and Wesleyan reflections that may significantly enhance our attempts at working toward alternatives to economic globalization. I hope to present a theology with a human face rather than a theology of mere intellectual engagement, theology for living rather than a theology for books.

1. THE PEOPLE'S BUDGET CAMPAIGN AND THE BASIC INCOME GRANT COALITION AS EXAMPLES OF LIVING THEOLOGY

The People's Budget Campaign (PBC) was conceived in 2000 as a joint campaign critically to engage the South African government on its budget choices and fiscal allocation. The three founder stakeholders are the Congress of South African Trade Unions (COSATU), the South African Council of Churches (SACC), and the South African NGO Coalition (SANGOCO). The churches' participation is defined by the search for economic justice and a pro-poor budget, advocating that governments spend more and more wisely on the social needs of the poor in order to redress the apartheid legacies of economic and social inequity. The Basic Income Grant Campaign is a sibling of the PBC and similarly advocates for poverty eradication by engaging government in the formulation of comprehensive social security policies, including a guaranteed minimum income, especially for the nearly 20 million South Africans who live on less than two U.S. dollars a day. These campaigns are accountable to church, labor, and civil society constituencies in South Africa.

In the vexed context of South Africa's integration into the global economy and its current guise of global capital expansion, Keith Vermeulen, working within the People's Budget Campaign and the Basic Income Grant Coalition, challenges us to revisit our Wesleyan heritage.[31] He interrogates various assumptions of neoliberal market economy and uses his understanding of Mr. Wesley's "means of grace" and "salvation by faith" to advocate on behalf of communities in South Africa that still bear the legacies of apartheid inequity. Interpreting our Methodist heritage from the underside of history, Vermeulen forces us to look at critical questions:

If we are saved by grace through faith to do good works as co-creators with God (Eph. 2:8-10), how is it possible to hand over an economic order to "the invisible hand of market forces"? Does not such moral distortion of market economy pose a clear challenge to the Creator's sovereignty as well as a subtle leverage for claims to divine inspiration of the current market economy? To what extent has a market economy that encourages the privatization of rights and social assistance encouraged the people called Methodists to renege on the option for the poor as an integral part of Wesleyan service through the means of grace? Has the "theology" of a market economy not contributed to an unnatural widening of the distances already promoted between the secular/sacred and public/private realms so rigorously held together in Mr. Wesley's life of Christian perfection? If we believe that Wesleyans promote the evangelical injunction of salvation and a divine-human partnership for the good of a renewed earth (Eph. 2:8-10), how do we then justify a distinction between salvation and the call on the saved to exercise stewardship over resources intended for the good of all creation, especially if such stewardship is a forbidden practice in a market economy?

If the earth is the Lord's and everything in it (Ps. 24:1), how do we accept an economic order based on scarcity and therefore inequitable distribution? And even if we practically must accept that market economics is the dominant economic model and that we are duty bound to participate therein, how do we deal with the growing inequity between rich and poor, developed and developing nations, and with its related problems such as debt, disease, and death? Can we find any biblical or theological justification for the idea that an economic order and globalization are value free? Recall Jesus' words that we can't serve two masters: God and mammon.

World Methodists would do well to attempt to address these questions as we seek to confirm our vocations and "serve the present age" by interrogating the assumptions that underlie global economic expansion and neoliberalism. Further considerations for engagement would be the nature of alliance building and cooperation with other sectors of civil society, the ecumenical movement and organized labor, like the call for debt cancellation, advocacy, and economic reforms as espoused by the Jubilee movement.

These activities are examples of how Wesleyans can make relevant Wesley's catholic spirit. We need to extend our understanding of Wesley's "parish" because challenging the order of global economics that denies life and degrades our humanity involves tasks that Wesleyans need to engage in order to be clear about the alternatives for God's economy. This, in my understanding, is what "evangelical economics" offers. Neoliberalism must not be allowed to define our vocation or the nature of our service in the world.

2. *UBUNTU/BOTHO: SALVATION FOR THE PEOPLE AND THE ECONOMIC SYSTEM*

We have already addressed the issue of Ubuntu/Botho in the context of economic justice in a global market economy. Suffice it here to add that the concept of Ubuntu/Botho can contribute to the vision of a life-affirming, just, and sustainable economy. This sense of human belonging, identity, and quality of relationships is further enhanced by Archbishop Emeritus Desmond Tutu when he refers to Ubuntu as "the essence of being human [which] embraces hospitality, caring about others, willingness to go the extra mile for the sake of another." When we add to these values the value of sharing, we may extend the depth of Wesley's catholic spirit by recognizing and co-opting the African way of life as Christian and Wesleyan and vice versa.

Perhaps it is the quality of Ubuntu in Mr. Wesley that has allowed Methodism to flourish on the African continent. If we accept this natural symbiosis, we will understand LenkaBula's connection of Botho/Ubuntu economics with an African and Wesleyan quest for a sustainable global economy and God's future economy. LenkaBula argues that Botho/Ubuntu is the basis for morality, cooperation, compassion, and communalism and, when embraced, enhances our ability to work toward the ideals of a more just society and world. Embedded in the concept are fundamental values and notions, such as solidarity with the vulnerable and marginalized, communal responsibility for the sustenance of life, and propensity to share with the less privileged rather than to promote an acquisitive society. Even in the midst of the scarcity, hardship, and degradation that Africans experience and continue to endure, LenkaBula believes that "Ubuntu has remained as a life, ethical, and social resource which African people continue to utilize for their sustenance. It is an ethic which provides a commendable schema of values to survive . . . despite colonialism, apartheid, wars and conflicts."[32]

When the chips are down and the ravages of a global economy based on consumerism, greed, and the extraction of every resource for profit hit home, it will not only be the African who is degraded of human status. Human degradation, on a global scale irrespective of where we come from, will be the reality. It is perhaps then that all may recognize the salvation qualities of Ubuntu—the heart of sustenance for African resilience—and that it has much to offer the twenty-first century, the rest of the world, and of course, the Wesleyan traditions and heritage.

3. Wesley's Catholic Spirit and the Olive Agenda

In more ways than one, big business and the global economy have assumed the role of promoting a "green agenda" by developing a culture of supply and demand on an abundance of resources, be it fossil fuels for energy or the supply of privatized water and global agribusiness for food. On the one hand, the assumption is that the earth's resources can best be exploited for the provision of human need while such provision may also generate a surplus of cash or profit. The scientific communities and the United Nations are in agreement that this model contributes to global warming and climate change and does *not* contribute toward sustainable development. I suggest that Wesleyans take heed of Wesley's inclusive and cooperative spirit for enhancing the dignity of humanity. For if our spiritualities and theologies do not contribute to the enhancement of human dignity and learn from Ubuntu, they may not be worth the effort. The recognition of cooperation with all God's people—the "household of God" (*oikos+mene*)—is integrated into the warm heart and extended hand. Integrated into these concerns would be the law of the household, the economy (*oikos+nomos*), based on the understanding that God is the ultimate owner and steward of the resources of the cosmos. The recognition that this household—"the people of God"—is called to care for creation and maintain its use for future generations is its ecology (*oikos+logos*). The ecumenical agenda has great benefit for taking on board the olive agenda defined by Steve de Gruchy in his address to the 2007 SACC National Conference, which featured the theme "Behold, I Make All Things New."[33]

In his address, de Gruchy proposes an "olive agenda" (that will take the "brown agenda" with its focus on poverty and the "green agenda" with its focus on the environment) to integrate economics with ecology, peace with justice, health with prosperity, democracy with tolerance that together hold a vision of God's economy. "What should be clear," says de Gruchy, "is that while both [brown and green agendas] are fundamentally right, taken in isolation from the other, each is tragically wrong—and thus we must restate our . . . concern to integrate economy as *oikos-nomos*, and ecology as *oikos-logos* in search of sustainable life on earth, *the oikos that is our only home*." I want to suggest that, taken in the spirit of Ubuntu/Botho, de Gruchy overstates his case. Neither is wrong, even in its own esteem.

One practical way of exploring the integrated olive agenda might be for God's people to develop poverty eradication strategies such as land provision for the poor, together with an exploration of the use of renewable energies—wind, wave, sun—in place of a continual reliance on fossil fuels (coal, uranium for nuclear energy, and even biofuels, which assume the use of earth that in Africa should be dedicated to raising food).

Suffice it to say that in the South African ecumenical agenda the future of God's newness relies on the philosophy of Ubuntu—and vice versa—as a philosophy for "humaneness" and human dignity. These, holding together the integrity of human development with God's created order, provide fertile ground for, and in fact the key to, unlocking the contemporary meaning of Wesley's catholic spirit and the doctrine of sanctification.

CONCLUSION

The abolition of slavery two hundred years ago is something without precedent in history. Yet the existence of millions of economically enslaved people around the world as a result of economic globalization is a scandal and major challenge for our time. Just as the abolition of slavery was an imperative for Christians in the eighteenth and nineteenth centuries, so I believe we need to have the same passion, commitment, and determination of the abolitionists if we hope to end the slavery created by global economic expansionism in our century.

Many economic and developmental scholars have warned and spoken out over the past decades against the systematic pillage, rape, and looting of the African continent's resources. They have been ignored or, in the case of Walter Rodney and others, had their lives snuffed out. Are we likely to witness the same denial and rejection of critiques of neoliberalism? Our theological reflection needs to unmask idolatry and remind us that God acts in human history through human activity. I would argue that we as Wesleyans need to develop mind-sets that challenge the doctrine of economic globalization that "there is no alternative" to neoliberal economics. An immediate project that comes to mind is the possible utilization of our Wesleyan resources in a joint effort with like-minded civil society organizations, for the purpose of lobbying our governments for macroeconomic choices that make clear provision of the basic necessities for the poor, marginalized, women, and children in our world. This attempt at exploring a living theology—small and incipient as the People's Budget and Basic Income Grant Campaigns in South Africa are—does not merely describe the distant suffering of others but integrates faith and works, and presents a model worth emulating on a continental and global scale.

As contemporary heirs of Mr. Wesley, we remind ourselves that our roots are firmly planted in the doctrine of sanctification; for this reason, "we were raised up, to spread Scriptural holiness throughout" our lands and to share in the momentous task of being "co-creators," agents of transformation for God's future in this world. It is only as we draw on our heritage and again link faith and works, pietism and social action, spirituality and political engagement that this future of God—a new world of justice, peace, and human security—will become a reality.

My life and ministry have been shaped by the vastness of God's abundant grace and salvation, which has creatively ebbed and flowed through my Wesleyan and African heritage. I am grateful for these heritages that have brought me to this time and place. I am of the firm conviction that our vocation and service "to the present age" are a call for transformative justice that goes beyond the fulfilling of rights. It is a moral, ethical, and theological imperative to be in solidarity with the poor while caring for the earth that God has placed in our care. Such a task is irrevocably bound up with discerning God's future, a future that calls us to be a different church for a different world. We live in an age pregnant with hope, where the new is waiting to be born. Our calling is to work together with all humanity to shape this different future.

CHAPTER SIX

CHRISTIAN PERFECTION: A METHODIST PERSPECTIVE ON ECCLESIOLOGY

Marjorie Hewitt Suchocki

It is time honored—traditional in the best sense of the word—to define the church in two parallel ways: the gathering of believers where the word of God is preached and the sacraments are duly administered, which speaks primarily to functions within the church, and the more ancient creedal formulation of the church as the one, holy, catholic, and apostolic people of God, which suggests an enduring and defining essence of the church. Perhaps ever since Albert Outler's provocative Oxford Institute lecture in 1962, however, Methodist theologians have struggled with the distinctiveness (or absence thereof) of a peculiarly Methodist understanding of the church.[1] The focus of many of our writings on the theme tends toward explicating the missional nature of a Methodist ecclesiology (for example, reforming the church and spreading scriptural holiness throughout the land) and applying that missional nature to the essence as well as function of the church. This is to say that there is a characteristic pragmatism to any Methodist ecclesiology.

My musings on Methodist ecclesiology flow from the theological work that has been most influential in my thinking as a process theologian, Wesley's *A Plain Account of Christian Perfection*.[2] I first read this marvelous little book during an airplane trip in April 1984, several months after I had become a United Methodist, and please do not think me trite by telling you that it strangely warmed my heart, because it simply did. I thought it the most exciting theological book I'd ever read, and it has shaped all my subsequent studies in Methodist theology, influenced my way of writing process theology, and certainly is central to my efforts here in suggesting that it offers a distinctively Methodist perspective on ecclesiology. That is, our self-understanding as Methodists and our contribution to ecumenical ecclesiology are to clarify the sense in which Christian perfection illumines the traditional formulations of the church.

To clarify my perspective on Wesley's doctrine of Christian perfection, I briefly summarize it as this: God created the world for the sake of the love that was possible for creation, a love mirroring God's own love, which is to say, love as the image of God. Love is essentially an active and intentional care for the well-being of the other. Well-being, in its turn, involves the use of all one's powers (physical, mental, emotional) to the glory of God. This brings us full circle because the glory of God is nothing other than the love of God, an active and intentional care for the well-being of the other. Because God intends this, it is really possible for us to be loving creatures (and this is where Wesley seems to me to be so distinctive). Christian perfection—that is, a life of love which is interchangeably love of God and creatures—is no carrot on a stick, no end-of-the-line reward at death's door, but an ever-present empowerment by the grace of the ever-present God. Precisely because this empowerment is for love, it is necessarily communal, creating interwoven webs of care for one another's well-being, so, of course, it is an important basis for any Methodist perspective on a doctrine of the church.

At this point I need also to clarify that for me there is a natural fusion between process and Wesleyan theologies. Both depend upon the efficacious omnipresence of God—and I think a case could be made that in both process and Wesleyan theologies, omnipresence is the most significant of the three traditional omni's assigned to God. Wesley's final words were, "The best of all is, God is with us."[3] The words undoubtedly refer to Wesley's experience of God's presence at that holy time, but the tenor of his life and thought is that God is indeed always present to creation; there is no place where God is not, regardless of whether there exists any creaturely consciousness of God's presence. The doctrine of Christian perfection entails a fundamental life stance attuned to the presence of God, a kind of holy assumption that takes omnipresence seriously, even for granted. And the presence of God is never passive but always active, which means that the presence of God is at the same time the continual availability of the grace of God. Since the grace of God flows from the love of God, grace is always adapted to the condition of the creature.

While phrased in different terminologies, all of the above also applies to process modes of thought. Existence by definition requires the ever-present creative power of God, not just once, long ago, whether in a "big bang" or otherwise, but everlastingly, moment by moment. Apart from the continuous and efficacious presence of God, there is nothing. Nothing whatsoever comes into existence without the attendant influence of God, called most infelicitously by Whitehead as "the initial aim," and more appropriately by Wesley as "grace." This aim, or grace, is adapted to the condition of the creature. Wesley, of course, described this adaptation in terms of prevenient, justifying, or sanctifying grace; Whitehead speaks more generally of the aim as adapted to the context and possibilities of the creature in every moment. Precisely because it is so adapted, it is an enabling aim, hence gracious.

But it is not a controlling aim. The creature must take that aim into account at its deepest level of becoming, finally becoming what it will within the parameters available to it. Insofar as the creature adopts/adapts the aim, it constitutes itself in light of its own personal and communal good, achieving God's gracious intent for it. The alternative is, of course, also possible. The becoming creature can refuse or distort God's influence, which is to constitute itself in ways that are less conducive to its own and the common good. In Wesleyan terms, grace is always given; grace is always resistible. But the omnipresence of God means that the refusal of grace cannot annul the continuous presence of God to every moment in the becoming creature's life, even though the creature can dull itself to God's presence.

Both process and Wesleyan theologies assume an essential responsiveness and therefore responsibility in creaturely existence. Wesley terms it "resistible grace"; process speaks of the power of the becoming occasion to subvert the influence of God. In both process and Wesley, grace is enabling—it is truly possible to respond positively to the grace of God. But grace is not forcing—it is truly possible to resist grace. Resistance cannot send God away, as if somehow God could no longer be present to the individual. But resistance builds up cumulative roadblocks that hinder the grace of God.

Process and Wesleyan theologies are intensely relational— Wesley because of the dominance of love, which is of all things most relational, and process because of its analysis that to exist at all is to be in relation to that which is other than the self. Existence is essentially and necessarily social.

And process and Wesleyan theologies are both transformation-al—Wesley because love is itself a transforming quality, continu-ously adapting to the condition of the loved one toward the increase of well-being and the building of community. Christian perfection is the process of being continuously formed in the image of God, participating in God's own love. It is of all things dynam-ic, not static. In process thought, God pushes the world toward its creative transformation into increasing intensities, which are dynamic interrelated communities of well-being. Wesley would call it love.

With this rather extended introduction, then, let us turn to the issue I have proposed: that Wesley's doctrine of Christian perfec-tion forms the bedrock of a Methodist perspective on ecclesiology. We first consider this in relation to the definition of the church in Article XIII as that "congregation of faithful men and women in which the pure Word of God is preached, and the sacraments be duly administered" (see the *Book of Discipline of The United Methodist Church*) and second in relation to the four traditional marks of the church. My remarks are intended to be suggestive rather than exhaustive since obviously a full development of this theme would require seven essays.

CHRISTIAN PERFECTION: WORD AND SACRAMENT

I have summarized Wesley's doctrine by saying that God creates the world for the sake of divine love, that the world is intended to mirror that love in its own ways, participating in God's love and thus glorifying God. In the middle of *A Plain Account*, Wesley fleshes this out a bit in his description of the ideal Adam.[4] Today we might take that ideal not as a past event from which we have fallen but as a goal toward which we should aim, enabled by the grace of God. Wesley says that all of Adam's powers—physical, affectional, intellectual—were to be fully developed in service to love. By implication, our formation in the image of God requires that we develop the fullness of our humanity—physical, affectional, intellectual—in the service of love.[5]

Wesley well notes that we exist within circumstances that limit what that fullness might be. We are, he asserts, "hedged in by outward circumstances."[6] Our physical development may be hindered by cerebral palsy, mental disorder, blindness, or some such limiting condition. Our affectional life may be hindered by childhood abuse; our intellectual developments will vary according to our different capacities. The norm is that we should grow into, that which is best fitted to us, that which is possible for us, and—most centrally—that this growth shall be guided by the norm of participation in the love of God. Our physical, affectional, and intellectual lives are channels of God's love for the particularities of the world, so that God's love infuses our love, and our love becomes a part of God's love.

Because Wesley develops the above in relation to Adam, one could be misled into considering this a very individualistic doctrine. But because Wesley considers Adam representative of humanity, and because the whole concept deals with love—the intentional care toward the well-being of others—we must recognize it as an essentially communal doctrine. Love cannot be love apart from that which is loved. Even potential love is not love until one's concern, one's very being, extends toward empathic caring for another. Simultaneously, to love is to be open to love, to be receptive to the empathic caring of others toward the self. Love necessarily creates community. In process terms, love builds upon the essential relationality of existence by responding empathically to others toward the end of mutual well-being. In Wesley's terms, God's very nature is this love; this care toward well-being is the foundation of God's creative work: "thy nature and thy name is Love."[7] We are called to participate in God's own love by receiving it, being formed by it, and endlessly giving it. Love is the energy of the universe, the creation of community, the enrichment of all aspects of becoming. Christian perfection is our participation in the love of God, which is at the same time our formation in the image of God.

If this is so, how can Christian perfection be separated from the functions of the church in preaching the gospel and administering the sacraments? Does it not provide the depth and the dynamic of both? And is it not so that, apart from communicating the love of God, in a depth sense neither preaching nor sacraments amount to anything? Since the love of God is the creative aim of God in creation, it clearly must inform our understanding of the preaching and sacramental functions of the church.

Preaching is for the sake of strengthening the community of believers in their several and communal ways of incarnating the love of God in their joint and their diverse circumstances. It involves a traditioning function, wherein "one generation proclaims the works of God to the next," to paraphrase Psalm 145. In this sense, word and sacraments make the past a present reality, so that tradition is a living participation in ancient faith. But both also have transformative functions, eschatological functions if you will, calling us to shape ourselves according to God's love here and now for the sake of what might yet be. The doctrine of Christian perfection suggests that the underlying force of past and future dimensions of word and sacrament is their role in the church's continual renewal in the image of God. Word and sacrament are both for the sake of increasing our active care for the well-being of those within and those beyond the community of faith. Both are means of incorporating us into God's love for the world.

I recognize that this appears to be a quite functional understanding of word and sacrament, but as a process Wesleyan, I cannot so neatly separate what a thing does from what a thing is. Consider: preaching is the act of expounding the gospel, whether through exegesis of biblical texts or through application of

Christian sensitivity to local circumstances. But if the gospel *is* the expressed love of God in Jesus Christ toward the well-being of the creature, then proclamation of the gospel *always* entails an influence toward our personal and communal participation in God's love, so that we severally and together mirror that love, channeling it to one another and to the world. God created us so that we might mirror God's love; this mirroring is accomplished through God's gracious influence and our response; God's influence is always contextual, taking account of where and when we are. The preached word is to explicate that which is happening all the time; it is the manifest word accompanying the hidden word of God's omnipresent activity within us. Hence preaching brings God's past activity in Christ into the present for the sake of the present community's deeper participation in the love of God. Preaching, then, is also participation in God's love.

Consider the sacraments of baptism and the Lord's Supper in relation to the doctrine of Christian perfection. We call them "means of grace," and that they are, but certainly not exclusively or exhaustively. Indeed, Wesley easily includes holy conversation, prayer, and class meetings as means of grace insofar as these also lead to the strengthening of the Christian's growth in love. However, there is a peculiarity to baptism and the Lord's Supper that sets them apart, for they uniquely pull the past and future into our present growth in love. Both explicitly refer to the manifestation of God with us in the incarnation, life, death, and resurrection of Christ; both are explicitly eschatological, referring to the fullness of God's purposes in creation. Both deal with the present constitution of the community of God's people as a manifestation of the love of God. Both involve the grace of God mediated through physical stuff within a community, and both pull God's "time" into our times and set our times within God's time. That is to say, both present an intersection of time and eternity.

Baptism and the Lord's Supper are by definition intensely communal acts. Baptism requires the participation of a community of faith, for an essential aspect of baptism is the community's vow to nurture the one baptized. Every educational program within the church is an extension of baptism, being a part of the fulfillment of that baptismal vow.

The Lord's Supper likewise requires the community of faith, for through this supper we co-communicate, realizing ourselves as together the body of Christ. All of this, however, tends toward a single purpose: creating us in the image of God, as a people who participate in the love of God receptively and actively. Apart from the love of the omnipresent God, calling us to participation in God's love, there are no sacraments within the church.

If Christian perfection is renewal in the image of God, and if the image of God is love, and if love is the intentional care for the full well-being—physical, affectional, intellectual—of the other, then the sacraments serve the end of Christian perfection.

Having said this, then, it would be foolish to leave this discussion of Christian perfection relative to word and sacrament without speaking of the church's mission in the world. Ecclesiology cannot be about the formation of a church as if it existed in and for itself. If the church exists to participate in the love of God, and if God loves the world, and if love cares for the fullness of well-being, then the church, which is strengthened in love through word and sacrament, necessarily expends itself in service to the needs of the world. These needs, in keeping with the doctrine of Christian perfection, deal with the physical, affectional, and intellectual well-being of persons and society, and the root of that well-being in the image of God.

How could it be otherwise? Wesley writes an interesting little paragraph near the end of *A Plain Account* that we all do well to memorize: "One of the principal rules of religion is, to lose no occasion of serving God. And since God is invisible to our eyes, we are to serve God in our neighbor, which God receives as if done to [Godself] in person, standing visibly before us."

If we participate in God's love, we will care intensely about the physical, affectional, and intellectual well-being of everyone and everything. For God does. Think about this in the fairly simple terms of your closest loves. To love someone is to care about the things that make for their well-being—their friends, their opportunities, their growth, their own loves. Love is such an expansive thing! If there is no greater love than God's love, then to say that "God so loved the world" means that God cares intensely about the well-being of each individual within the world. If God loves that other, and we participate in the love of God, then perforce we also must love that other. Jesus' words—"love your enemies, do good to those who hate you"—take on an awesome meaning in light of the doctrine of Christian perfection. We love precisely because God loves; therefore, we cannot say that love goes so far and no farther.

Truthfully, no finite individual can have an active love for everything, but the church is not an individual. It is community, and in and through the community as a whole we participate in the love of God in myriad ways. To view both word and sacrament as that which tends toward the building of the community in the image of God is to view both as intensely missional, calling and empowering us to active love for the world. Mission, then, is not something added on to word and sacrament; it is part and parcel of word and sacrament. Because word and sacrament, as means to our growth in Christian perfection, are themselves rooted in Christian perfection.

Should you ask whether I have woven any particularly process perspectives into my development here, perhaps taking you unaware, the answer would be yes (though I would rather take you "aware" than "unaware"). My process assumption is that God guides us within the depths of who we are at every second of our being, bending every element of our past and our peculiar situation in the present toward our communal good. I have called this a "whispered word," since it is deeper than consciousness. The preached word and the tangible sacramental words are manifest words through which God intensifies that whispered word, strengthening our capacity to be formed in God's image. Hence both word and sacrament are means of grace, used of God toward our growth in love and therefore intensifying our responsiveness to God and one another in the formation of community.

CHRISTIAN PERFECTION AND THE MARKS OF THE CHURCH

One, holy, catholic, and apostolic church—so speaks the creed. To view these marks under the rubric of Christian perfection gives them a far less divisive character than too often obtains. The unity of the church makes this perhaps most plain.

Often the unity of the church has been framed in terms of universal communion, so that no Christian is barred from the Lord's Supper in any congregation, be it Protestant, Catholic, or Orthodox. At other times the unity of the church has been interpreted as organizational, so that in and through the episcopacy, or papacy, the church receives its unity. Yet another variation perceives unity as agreement as to doctrine. But in all these cases, the most prominent aspect of unity is that it isn't. The definitions divide rather than unify the various modes of Christian community. The doctrine of Christian perfection, of course, roots the unity of the church in love. By extension, one can also say that the unity of the church exists through prayer, but we first treat unity and love.

Wesley's relevant passages are in his advices to those seeking Christian perfection, found in the latter part of this small work. His first advice, dealing with pride, is as relevant as his specific advices dealing with schism, for he defines pride as the refusal to learn from those who differ from oneself. In the advices regarding schism, he cautions Methodists to expect controversy and differences of theological opinion. Ecumenically, we see his principle extended to that "olive branch" offered to the Romans. And it is certainly in his sermon "A Catholic Spirit." Christian perfection suggests that the unity of the church, whether within a congregation or denomination, or ecumenically, is fundamentally love. Further, this love—this unity—is expressed through goodwill, prayer, and works of mercy. And it depends upon theological diversity.

The odd implication is that theological conformity—that which has sometimes been held to be essential for any real unity within the church—actually functions against unity. The reason is found within Wesley's advices, as noted above. Controversy actually has a positive function within the church, for it becomes a means toward growth in Christian love. The reason is both complex and simple: God loves each person personally and contextually; God wills the well-being of the persons and the community as a whole. We love God, and in so doing, we participate in God's love for the world. Therefore, regarding the other as the beloved of God, we too are called to be oriented toward the other's well-being.

The catch is that we too often think that the well-being of the other entails their becoming just like us. But Wesley cautions us in *A Plain Account* to recognize fully our fallibility: we cannot always reason correctly, and therefore we must expect to make mistakes. There must always be the question hanging upon any theological or ethical controversy: perhaps the other is right, even though I most heartily do not think so. But since by definition we do not know when we make mistakes—else we would not be so prone to make them—we must hold our opinions with some humility. The God whom we are so sure has given us light also gives light to the other.

You can see how this circumstance enhances growth in Christian love. It means the one who differs from us, even vehemently, cannot be considered alien, and must even be considered as a possible means of enlightenment. "You have need to be taught . . . by the weakest preacher in London, yea, by all," says Wesley, and he includes among those from whom we must learn several who disagreed strongly with Wesley himself. Differences of theological or ethical or organizational opinion become occasions of grace, of entering into God's love for the one who differs with us, and therefore regarding that one with respect and curiosity rather than anger or dismissal.

A further entailment is that extending love toward those who differ with us strengthens our capacity to participate in God's love. A humble analogy is the attempt to build one's muscle strength through exercise. Loving those who are like ourselves is like exercising our capacity to love by lifting feathers. But loving those who are unlike ourselves is like exercising our capacity to love by lifting weights. The latter, not the former, strengthens our capacities—for it is easy to love that which is like, and far harder to love that which is different. But God is as present to and is as caring toward the one who differs from us as toward the one who is like us. Participating in God's love requires our openness to those who differ from ourselves as occasions of grace.

Such unity is not easy to achieve. But the doctrine of Christian perfection claims that it is truly possible for us to participate in God's love: it is possible for us to love those unlike ourselves. It does not plunge us into indifferentism; that would hardly be

Wesleyan. And it certainly does not squelch theological arguments or lead to conferences in which no one disagrees with another. Quite to the contrary: just as the other may be light to us, we may possibly be light to the other. But it is God's love in which we participate, not God's omniscience: we are called to dig deeply into the depths of our faith, to formulate it as carefully as possible—but always as we press our point, our participation in God's love means that we offer our arguments, opinions, or judgments in loving regard for the other's worth—and possible correctness.

Obviously, loving does not always entail liking, and the unity of the church depends on loving one another, not necessarily liking one another. I believe that the highest form of love involves the emotional warmth that we associate with liking, since it involves the fullness of our physical, affectional, and intellectual selves in orientation toward the other's well-being. But at its basic level, to love means to care about the well-being of the other, whether or not we have a liking for that other. I mention this only because sometimes in the hurtfulness of our human situation, persons are severely damaged by others: a rapist, a molester, a murderer, a character assassinator. To like those who have so damaged one may not be possible, but to love those is possible. Clearly, the well-being of the other includes transformation from raping, molesting, or whatever form of harm has been inflicted; one can will such well-being for the other, and in and through that transformation, will their flourishing. Loving can transcend the particularities of liking. Even within the church, in our disagreements we can disparage rather than respect one another, making the liking of friendship very difficult. But we can love those who despitefully use us, willing and acting toward their well-being, and so participate in God's unending love for that other.

Love, then, is the basis of the unity of the church, even in the midst of theological, ethical, or organizational controversies. Hence Wesley can hold out his "olive branch to the Romans" and reason with the Calvinists. But it also follows that prayer is the unity of the church, and this from love. Simply put, prayer is our openness to God, our communion with the source of all love, our responsiveness to the omnipresent God. Prayer opens us to participation in the love of God. And when it is hard for us truly to will the well-being of the other because of antagonism or dislike, our recourse is to pray for that well-being, uniting us with the other in God's care. In the process of praying for the other, God's love works in our hearts, forming us not so much according to our injuries but according to God's love. It is possible through prayer to begin to mirror in some degree the fullness of God's love for the ones for whom we pray. Prayer is participatory; hence prayer follows the lines of love.

The image of Christian perfection as the unity of the church, then, does not conceive of differing denominations as the brokenness of the church, even though the controversies initiating the denominations were unloving or schismatic. The unity of love requires differentiation and can even bear with strong theological differences over who may participate in the Lord's Supper that exclude some Christians from the Lord's table in some church settings. The response of Christian perfection is to regard the other, looking for the well-being achieved within that different context; it is to pray for the other; it is to engage the other in Christian conversation so as to understand one another's perspective, with the expectation that each perspective will be offered persuasively and, ideally, with openness to learning from the other. Unity does not require that we become like the other or the other like us. Unity requires that we participate in God's love for the other. And I think it an interesting oddity attendant upon this view that sometimes when we have met together ecumenically, bemoaning our disunity, we are in fact exercising the unity of Christian perfection: participating in God's love for one another.

I have perhaps belabored the point, since I ought not to treat holiness, catholicity, and apostolicity in equal length. But brevity might be sufficient, given our joint familiarity with Christian perfection. Holiness is a different way of speaking about our participation in the love of God. It is therefore personal and communal simultaneously, and is that quality of communal life wherein our worship services open us communally to the love of God so that as community, we extend God's love to the world's physical, affectional, and intellectual well-being. Our hospitals, our schools, our distributions of aid, our ways of nurturing, are all extensions of holiness, since each is a communal expression of participation in the love of God.

Holiness cannot be restricted to works of mercy, since these works follow from holiness, which is love of God and therefore love of neighbor. The holiness of the church is manifest in the regard of the members one for the other, and this regard in turn is rooted in the love of God: God's love for us, and our responsive love for God. Again, I must stress that to love God is to participate in God's love, in which case it is impossible for love not to be communal. Love of God necessitates the continual creation of the community. Holiness, as the love of God, is the lifeblood of the church.

Catholicity recognizes the diverse communities of Christian faith, adapted by the grace of God to various cultures, but all infused with God's love, all open to being shaped by God's love, all open to living God's love within and beyond the church. Wesley speaks of the catholicity of the church in terms of its geographical adaptations, but he is also at some pains to note that catholicity includes diversity of doctrine and modes of worship as well as diversity of location (see for example his sermon "Of the Church").

The catholicity of the church relativizes every form of the church. That is, if differences are embraced within catholicity, then no single form of the church is the norm or judge of the others. The diversity given to strengthen love within a single congregation or annual conference within our Methodism is multiplied exponentially in light of the ecumenical church. Ideally, this diversity of forms within the catholicity of the church is an astonishing occasion for the practice of love, not only toward one another across our differences, but together in works of mercy throughout our globe. Ecumenical organizations such as Bread for the World witness to the root of catholicity in Christian perfection.

Apostolicity is not only our standing within the two-thousand-year-old tradition of Christianity as mediated through our Scriptures and through the diverse writings of these centuries, but it is in fact our contemporary participation in the ongoing tradition. Christian perfection is as applicable to apostolicity as to the other marks of the church, revealing the necessarily witnessing nature of participation in divine love. The love of God cannot be contained; participation in God's love likewise has an essentially giving nature, a telling forth that continually replicates the living message of the gospel throughout the ages.

Apostolicity is the living witness to the resurrection power of God in every human circumstance; as such, we are all eyewitnesses of the resurrection. The love of God has a transforming power gracing us to deal with the various forms of death that afflict us, the tombs that would bury us while we yet live. Christian perfection is the experience of the transforming love of God that offers personal and social resurrections even in the midst of our tragedies. Our experiences of God's resurrecting power are continuous with the apostolic witness, forming our present witness. Thus Christian perfection informs the apostolicity of the church, making it a contemporary as well as historic proclamation.

As Methodists, we affirm the church as that gathering of faithful men and women where the pure word of God is preached and the sacraments are duly administered. We affirm the unity, holiness, catholicity, and apostolicity of the church. As such, we do not proclaim a distinctive doctrine of the church, nor should we. We participate in the whole people of God, which surpasses any particular denomination—no matter how loved! Nor does any particular body within the whole people of God have the distinctive privilege of offering *the* doctrine of the church, to which all others must conform. Rather, we are all called to recognize the one, holy, catholic, and apostolic church, which is the gathering of faithful people where the word is preached and sacraments administered. As distinctive bodies within the whole people of God, we have the duty to probe the peculiar perspective on God's grace that has been given to us, and to offer that perspective for the enrichment of others. We do so not to force our doctrines upon them, for this would go quite contrary to the very love of God we espouse. Rather, we offer them as gifts to be taken or left as deemed fit by our brother/sister participants. And likewise, our task is to appreciate the particular perspectives offered by those other recipients of the grace of God through Jesus Christ, discerning what it is in the gift that God would have us receive. I submit that as Methodists, we offer to the whole people of God the gift of a Wesleyan account of Christian perfection—the love of God informing our hearts and lives, so that we become channels of God's love within and beyond our several communities. No community is a stranger to the love of God. But Wesley's conviction that by God's grace we are continuously renewed in this image, so that now in this place and time it is possible to live God's love, is a message of hope to enliven the whole people of God in our own and, indeed, in every age.

Baptism is not something reduced to happening "once" in our lives. Truly, we are initiated into baptism at an identifiable event, but that into which we are baptized is the body of Christ, the people of God, the fellowship of believers in the Spirit; we are baptized into an ongoing condition that necessarily entails the loving, shaping, nurturing response of the community. For Wesley, baptism is the "cleansing grace" of God, leading progressively to the justifying and sanctifying grace of God, but this is to say that God graces us according to our need and our condition. The baptismal condition is the surrounding community of those pressing on to Christian perfection, who as mirrors of God's love, care for the personal and communal well-being of the one baptized. As Luther so famously said to his perceived opponent, the devil, "I *am* baptized," not "I *was* baptized." Baptism initiates our everlasting condition of participation in God's love through Christ. "Remember your baptism, and be thankful" is analogous to the anamnesis of the Lord's Supper, recalling us to our deepest condition. Baptism is constant communion with God in Christ.

Even so, in reference to the Lord's Supper, constant communion does indeed entail frequent participation in the Lord's Supper, but there is a deeper dimension in that the supper *is* (and not represents only) our participation in Christ and therefore one another, for we are in Christ severally, relationally, personally, communally. The visible and tangible communion of bread and wine is the manifestation of that which is in time, but deeper than time, insofar as we participate in the ever-living love of the omnipresent God given to us through Christ. It is a constant communion in the shaping love of God.

These forms of constant communion—prayer, baptism, Lord's Supper—open us to our participation in God, and therefore in one another. That is, opening ourselves to the pervasive influence of God is necessarily opening ourselves to participating in God's love, and therefore to our increase in love. But to participate in

God's love is necessarily to participate in God's love for others as well as ourselves. It is probably too obvious to belabor, but God's love, while personal, is never private; it is always communal: God so loved the world. To love God is to participate in God's love for the world. This is why Wesley can say, "To love and serve God is the principal rule of all religion. And since God is invisible to our eyes, but our neighbor is not, we are to love God in our neighbor, which God receives unto God's own self as standing visibly before us." We love God by caring for the well-being of our neighbor. Thus growth in the love of God is necessarily communal. Christian perfection, as renewal in the image of God, necessarily binds persons communally into care for and of one another. In Christ, it is the continuous formation of the church.

CHAPTER SEVEN

HUMAN RIGHTS, VOCATION, AND HUMAN DIGNITY

Robin W. Lovin

I

One of the most important developments in law and morality during the twentieth century was that the idea of *human rights* became the universal language of political ethics. In the aftermath of two world wars, the notion that every person is entitled to certain basic human rights became the touchstone by which the actions of individuals and nations could be evaluated.[1] These rights include classic Enlightenment entitlements such as freedom of religion, freedom to form your own ideas about politics and government, the protection of life and liberty, and protection against persecution because of religion, ethnicity, or origins. In addition, the twentieth-century concept of human rights includes rights to the resources that make a free and secure life possible—fair wages and decent working conditions; basic needs for food, shelter, and health care; and access to education and opportunities that make a free and secure life meaningful.[2]

These requirements are summed up in the concept of "human dignity." Human beings, as such, deserve respect that goes beyond mere obedience to rules and sets them above the other things we value. Persons cannot be subordinated to ideologies, sacrificed for causes, or destroyed by the workings of markets, movements, or laws. They cannot be reduced to what they can produce or valued in terms of their place in a social hierarchy. The most basic political idea in an age of human rights is that persons as such must be protected and respected, by governments, and by other institutions and individuals.[3]

These ideas have been especially important since they were made central to the United Nations' Universal Declaration of Human Rights in 1948. Since that time, governments have been obliged to explain themselves in terms of these rights, whatever their aims or political philosophies might be. Regimes have had to pay at least lip service to them, even if they had no intention of honoring them in practice. Minimal respect for human rights has become a criterion for acceptance in the international community. It separates rogue states and failed states from legitimate governments that are entitled to a place among the nations of the world.

In the concept of human dignity, there is an echo of the Christian belief that genuine love for God requires love for all our neighbors just because they are God's children and not for anything that they might do or believe. Religious participation was central to the formulation of these principles of human dignity that have become the basis for international human rights. Ecumenical Protestant social ethics began shaping these ideas into a coherent system in the 1930s, and the strategizing of American and British church leaders, especially, pushed these questions to the top of the crowded agenda of the new United Nations organization after the Second World War.[4] They understood these political ideas to be deeply rooted in Christian tradition, but they also saw the importance of framing a *universal* declaration in broadly human terms, stressing the requirements of human dignity and minimizing claims about where those requirements come from and why they are authoritative. Thus, secular philosophers and political theorists were able to endorse the Universal Declaration of Human Rights and provide arguments for its validity. Even representatives of other religious traditions, though they were far less visible in that late-colonial era than they would be today, found reasons to support this document distilled from the key traditions of European religion and law. The result was a practical agreement on the specified rights with no consensus on the underlying principles. The negotiators regarded this practical agreement amidst ideological differences as a remarkable achievement.[5]

II

The Universal Declaration and the thoughts that went into it remain central to the theory of human rights and to international law on human rights to this day. But the practice of human rights has become problematic. The more than sixty years since the Universal Declaration was adopted have been marked by violations on a vast scale and by carefully crafted exceptions that allow even the staunchest supporters of the *idea* of human rights to exempt their countries from particular provisions or to escape the jurisdiction of international bodies that might begin to make these provisions a reality. The United States, in particular, seems to have been committed across the last several administrations in both political parties to the conviction that international human rights doctrine could not possibly require our country to do anything that it was not already going to do anyway.

In view of this very mixed record, we must conclude that the agreement on a list of basic rights that the world community celebrated in 1948 has not had the practical effect that its authors hoped for and expected. With no shared principles by which to understand the Universal Declaration, it has become impossible to say what it would require, given the new realities of a globalized economy, international terrorism, failed states, and the end of the cold war.

In the face of violence and militant fundamentalist movements in many religious traditions, some also question whether religion deserves a place at the table when human rights are discussed.[6] To these critics, the religious truth seems to require a kind of absolutism that makes it impossible to respect the rights of those who disagree or who fail to see the truth with the clarity that the true faith requires. From this point of view, it is best to get on with the creation of a purely secular system of law and rights. Archaic language about persons being equal in the sight of God or receiving their rights as part of God's creation can no longer do any useful work, and people who use that language may undermine the human rights they claim to support. Moving forward with a purely secular system of law and rights may, in fact, require restrictions on public expressions of religious devotion or public display of religious symbols. From this perspective, it is time for the concept of secular, nonreligious authority that has been part of every modern system of government to develop into a genuine *secularism.* Religious beliefs and practices can still be acknowledged, but they must become completely private, no different from any other personal preferences, and if they survive at all, they must do so without public support or recognition.

Others see the same developments, but they read the signs of the times quite differently. It is not the rise of militant religion that disturbs them but the failure of secular politics. They are increasingly inclined to treat the traditions of secular democracy as morally bankrupt and incapable of supporting the respect for persons that is supposed to be the distinctive contribution of democracy to political life.[7] "Human rights" for these thinkers is one of those dangerous Enlightenment abstractions against which Bishop Willimon warns us.[8] An earlier generation of theologians who devoted such energy to framing universal declarations about human rights was simply confused. They had mistaken Enlightenment individualism for a narrative that can actually form a moral community. Persons have identity and responsibility in that kind of community, and they cannot really respect one another on the basis of a list of disembodied "rights."

Theologians who question the language of rights do not support the new forms of religious militancy emerging in various parts of the world. In fact, they tend to be pacifists who want to draw a sharp line of distinction between the community of faith and any community that is held together by power and created by violence. But they claim to be able to explain why liberal democracy seems unable to get a hold on the imagination of people around the world who see their identity primarily in religious terms. People who define their identity in religious terms do not think of themselves as individuals possessed of abstract rights that they look to a secular government to enforce, nor can they frame whatever hopes they have for global community in terms of a set of universal rights to which everyone is entitled. If they are to become supporters of peace and dignity, it will have to be in terms drawn from their traditions of faith.

The result is a world of religion and politics that is quite different from the world the religious activists after the Second World War expected us to be living in by the beginning of the twenty-first century. The theologians and church leaders who pressed for a Universal Declaration of Human Rights supposed that by the beginning of the twenty-first century, democratic governments based on respect for individual rights would be ascendant everywhere. They expected that rational religion would be the natural ally of these democratic governments, lending moral seriousness to their political efforts and shaping an international order in which human rights would provide a neutral standard against which every political system might be measured. Those midcentury Christian activists were optimists, but they were not utopians. They expected that the extension of human rights into more traditional societies would be controversial and that the assertion of human rights against authoritarian governments would be resisted. They expected the adoption of the Universal Declaration of Human Rights to serve as the starting point for a long historical development in which declared rights would become global realities. What they did not expect was a world in which Christian theology would be divided over whether the language of human rights makes any sense as a starting point for political ethics.

Nevertheless, that is where we find ourselves. The commitment to human rights that was supposed to be the starting point for a new international order now marks a point of division, both within and between theology and politics.

III

For those of us who see the questions in theological terms, the disputes at the beginning of the twenty-first century seem oddly reminiscent of controversies within sixteenth-century Protestantism.

Christianity has been around for a long time—far longer than the systems of modern politics—and it seems that whenever the conditions of politics change fundamentally, we are forced back to some basic questions about how faith relates to power. Today, the issues of globalization and the future of the nation-state raise for us all over again a dispute that was played out at the beginning of the modern era, when the church had to figure out its relation to emerging secular politics for the first time. In that controversy, the new Protestant movement was internally divided between those who wanted to accept secular authority on its own terms and those who thought that Christians should distance themselves from it as much as possible. It is a difference expressed most clearly in the conflicts between Luther and the Anabaptists. Luther's followers saw themselves bound to society by a common need for peace and order. The Anabaptists saw Christian peace as a distinctive kind of order, which creates its own distinctive communities.

If you learned your church history as long ago as I did, you probably learned a version of the story in which Luther, Calvin, and what is sometimes called the "magisterial Reformation" triumphed, and the Mennonites, Brethren, and others who made up what is sometimes called the "radical Reformation" lost. They became a minority report within the European and North American Christianity that developed subsequently.

But if you learned Christian ethics more recently than that, you know that the pacifist perspective of the radical Reformation has been renewed in the work of contemporary authors like John Howard Yoder, who found the prevailing ideas of the magisterial Reformation an unsatisfactory compromise between the demands of the gospel and the requirements of political expediency.[9] So the issues of the sixteenth century are alive in a new way at the beginning of the twenty-first, and while the disagreements are not as violent as they were in the original controversy, it is almost as difficult to find common ground between the two positions. As often happens in theological disputes, Methodists can be found on both sides of the question, arguing their cases with equal vigor, and with equal conviction that their position represents the central values of the Wesleyan tradition.

Wesley himself might find the whole argument somewhat confusing, since his political theology tended to be drawn more from the relationship between royal and religious authority in the Anglican establishment rather than the sharper controversies between church and secular authority in continental Protestantism, and this not so much out of strong conviction as from his tendency to continue Anglican ways of thinking except where he saw a specific need to change them. As the Methodists became more clearly separated from the Church of England, Wesley had to defend their rights to preach, hold worship, and maintain chapels, but these were legal claims particular to the provisions of English law that did not elaborate themselves into a fully developed Methodist political theology.

Beyond his interest in rights that he thought he was legally entitled to claim for his societies, Wesley was certainly no advocate of modern ideas of natural rights, or what the French Revolution would shortly call the "rights of man."[10] He acknowledged the slave's claim to freedom as a "natural right," but he focused on the irony of slaveholders and slave traders who claim their own rights while denying freedom to others. Nor was the other Wesley wordsmith, brother Charles, any more inclined toward these political ideas. In a humorous poem "To Dr. Boyce," Charles asks the musician William Boyce to assist with the musical education of his son, describing his plea as "a petition of natural right."[11] The literary occasion was lighthearted, but the language is nonetheless revealing. The Wesleys knew the language of natural rights. It was all around them. But they made little use of it unless they were being humorous or ironical, or inveighing against someone else's moral contradictions. Certainly, their idea of rights was not theological.

Wesley strongly opposed slavery, not because he believed that "all men are created equal," but because he believed that the slave, like everyone else, has a soul that can be addressed, claimed, and redeemed by God.[12] Thus the slave, like everyone else, needs the freedom to respond to the word of grace proclaimed. The equality that Wesley understood was evangelical, not political, and he probably would have understood claims to human dignity on behalf of sinners in need of conversion as a positive hindrance to the reception of the gospel.

IV

Wesley sought to convert sinners rather than to make them acquainted with their rights. But looking back on the Methodist movement, we can say that one point where theology connects with sociology is that when you speak to people as though they were capable of having a relationship with God, they will indeed begin to enter into that relationship, and in very large numbers. No one at the beginning of the eighteenth century would have predicted from social facts of the time the transformation that religious revivals would make in the social fabric of Britain and her North American settlements. Indeed, what one might have expected was the deadening of the masses that was the first effect of the industrial and agricultural transformations in Britain during this time. One might have expected that working people, cut loose from ancestral homes and ancient customs, would suffer the fate predicted by Parson Malthus and be reduced to a level of subsistence living that made them mere instruments of the productive processes in which they labored. Or at least, one might have expected that to go on until it reached the point predicted by Marx, at which the impoverished proletariat would constitute so large a part of the population that the emerging capitalist system would collapse under its own weight.

But indeed what happened instead was the emergence of a relatively prosperous working class, which in due time became the Victorian middle class.[13] Economic forces made this social transformation possible, but the changes went along with personal and moral transformations that made that middle class more religious and more moral than the mass of the population had probably ever been before. People became more moral, more family-oriented, better educated, and better organized, and at least through the early part of the nineteenth century, you could summarize all those changes by saying that people became more Methodist.

In the process, they acquired in practice a dignity something like the personal discipline, capacity for decision, and self-direction that human rights doctrine attributed to them in theory.[14] They might have been surprised to hear that this dignity was something that they just had, *a priori*, since many of them worked quite hard to maintain the sober and industrious habits on which that dignity and their way of life seemed to depend, and they relied on God every day for that discipline; but they would probably have agreed at least that this dignity was not something that any *human* authority had given them or could take away from them.

This dignity was also, for many of them, closely related to a sense of vocation. God had not only summoned them to conversion but had sent them back into life with a calling, with unique responsibilities and obligations that had more to do with making a faithful response to God's mercy than with meeting social expectations. These callings reflected both a unique, personal relationship to God and the more fluid nature of social relationships in the rapidly changing world of the eighteenth century. Methodists were not called to a fixed place in a social hierarchy, like the medieval "estates" or the Lutheran "orders" that defined one's vocation as a member of a class of persons with permanent, unchanging duties and limitations. Methodists had the more open-ended calling to earn all one can, save all one can, and give all one can, beginning in the particular place in life where God has found one. Living up to that calling demanded constant effort and great self-discipline, but it might well take one to a place in society quite different from where one started.[15]

Perhaps most important of all, this dignity included the capacity to create the institutions necessary to sustain it. Methodists on both sides of the Atlantic were famous for their *religious* organization, for class meetings, circuits, and conferences. But all of these religious organizations developed their characteristic forms of social support, emergency assistance, and political training too. Methodists went on to establish publishing houses, orphanages, schools, and colleges. Often these were founded—and continue to this day—with an explicit connection to the church, but Methodists as individuals were also highly skilled in forming business, civic, and cultural organizations that gave form and permanence to their visions of the possibilities God had opened to them.

Methodists, non-Anglican "dissenters," and other evangelicals were perhaps the most effective participants in the social changes that took place over nearly two centuries from the English Revolution of 1688 through the American Civil War, as well as their greatest beneficiaries. It is worth remembering that they accomplished these things largely outside the established channels of political and economic power. These politically and socially marginal people on both sides of the Atlantic found ways to make themselves wealthier, better educated, and more effective in their philanthropy than the elites who initially regarded them with such suspicion. By the time they began to join those elites, they had their own ideas about what made a good society. Where Luther and the magisterial Reformation had emphasized the importance of order in times of dissolution and conflict, John Wesley emphasized practical collaboration on shared goods that helped people be virtuous as well as orderly. If the initial logic of the Radical Reformation favored withdrawal from the wider society, Wesley thought it was essential to the Methodist calling that "the providence of God has so mingled you together with other men." In that way, "whatever grace you have received of God may through you be communicated to others; that every holy temper, and word, and work of yours may have an influence on them also."[16] Methodists had a strong sense of how much they had in common with other sober and industrious people and how much they had to offer to those who were neither sober nor industrious.

These marginal Methodists eventually became part of the social center, but the ways they lived their faith continued to provide those on the margins with tools for understanding their situation, exercising some control over their lives, and even influencing the direction of the wider society. This was especially true in America, where quite beyond the intentions of the now mainstream Methodists, and in some cases against their active resistance, the institutional models that Methodists had created became available to the very groups that some of their descendants tried to exclude, expel, or control. African Americans after the Civil War, European immigrants in the late nineteenth century, and women in the early twentieth century all found the model of local organization, personal accountability, and a commitment to mutual assistance to be the key to a better life and, ultimately, the key to political empowerment. African American churches, colleges, and businesses replicated, in their distinctive ways, the successes of the early Methodists a century before.

Keeping this historic social vocation of Methodism in perspective is important. The story of Methodist discipline and prosperity now has to be seen in a global context. The discipline may have been Methodist, but the prosperity depended in part on systems of colonial and postcolonial exploitation. Methodists were carrying away their wealth from some of the same people to whom they were carrying the gospel.[17] The fact that they did not fully understand the economics of this relationship may excuse them of hypocrisy, but it does not change the reality of the relationships. It also does not excuse us in the North Atlantic world from responsibility for understanding what our ancestors could not, and for dealing responsibly with the long-term results of the realities they created.

Precisely because these realities have created a quite different social world in Africa, parts of Asia, and in Latin America, we cannot use the historic Wesleyan models that I have described in any simple and direct way in those places. The worlds are completely different, as Bishop Mattos reminds us.[18] Indeed, the worlds are completely different for us in the North Atlantic world too. In recounting the successes of the Wesleyan model in its own time and place, I would not want to be misunderstood as prescribing that we imitate it today. At least since 1932 in the United States and since 1945 in Britain, we have understood the relationship between persons and society and the social responsibilities of government in very different terms from those that prevailed in John Wesley's world, and the notion that we could solve today's problems with Wesley's economics is about as practical as trying to run a medical mission according to the advice found in his *Primitive Physic*. We would quite properly be shut down by the government for doing something similar today, and the fact that governments sometimes suggest churches could solve the problem of poverty illustrates that governments can be as confused as churches about the difference between strategy and understanding.

What we gain from the Methodist history of social transformation that is still valid today is not strategy but understanding. It is an understanding of the social conditions that make for human dignity and an understanding that we have a vocation to create those conditions with all those who share our society, whether or not they share our faith.

V

Methodism in the eighteenth and nineteenth centuries, when it was most influential and most effective, did not create a political theology, but it developed a substantial body of political experience that carries us beyond the oppositions of the Reformation era and reconnects us with the contemporary questions about the future of human rights on a global scale. What emerges clearly from the political experience of the Methodist movement is that human dignity is not an idea but a lived reality. It becomes possible to see persons endowed with unique dignity and possessed of specific rights that enable them to maintain that dignity once they have places where they can experience rights and dignity, and where other people who have eyes to see can observe the transformation at work.

Those who first attempted to create an international order based on human rights, beginning with the Universal Declaration of 1948, assumed that a consensus that was sufficient to establish a basis in positive international law was the main thing required to begin the process of making human rights available and effective on a global scale. In a world that had almost been destroyed by the power of modern states, it was perhaps inevitable that religious and secular leaders at the middle of the twentieth century would look to nations united by their various commitments to universal principles of human rights to create a different kind of world order. They were, in any case, operating with an idea of secular authority that Christians and others had largely accepted since the Reformation era, in which the authority of law, adopted for whatever reasons, is the starting point for order.

But the movements that created the modern democracies understood in practice that human dignity requires social reality before it can be made a political and legal reality. Their view of society was more pluralistic—not a dichotomy of church and state, Christian community and secular authority, but a variety of social settings in which Christians live out their callings alongside their neighbors. The variety of callings creates a pluralistic politics, in place of the dualisms of secular and spiritual, or public and private. Clive Marsh, in his explorations of contemporary Christology, has written of the need to carry the reality of Christ into the diversity of social relationships—family, friends, work, and politics.[19] That insight, drawn in part from the work of Faith and Order in British Methodism, is a reminder of the important role that earlier Methodists played in creating that diversity. Methodists have had less to say about church and state than some other Protestants because they have been busy creating a society that consists of more than just church and state.

This vocational pluralism assumes that agreement on particular human goods is possible apart from agreement on theology. Shared experience of evils overcome and goods sustained shows that moral meanings do not completely depend on a shared narrative of faith. People who want to fight disease, educate children, or make music together discover that they can do it across very different cultures and very different understandings of what the ultimate destiny of human life may be. They will sometimes stop doing it if religious or political authorities tell them that it is a bad idea, for theological or for constitutional reasons, but this vocational pluralism grew up very naturally, despite religious differences, and sometimes even in the face of religious hostility. The same experiences are repeated today on a global scale, across even larger gaps of faith and culture, and it is important to develop an understanding of politics that takes seriously these cross-cultural, cross-religious experiences. These experiences are the social realities that must precede political agreement on human rights.

This is the legacy of the Methodist movement to our contemporary understanding of human rights and human dignity. It is not a model for dealing with the more complex realities of global economics that we live with today. It is not a Wesleyan plan of action that we might try to imitate. Rather, what we receive from Wesley and those early Methodists is a pluralistic understanding of politics and society: human goods exist in the forms that people create and maintain in concrete social situations, in their interactions with one another across all the lines of race, religion, ethnicity, and class that initially divide them. There are various ways to understand these human goods in relationship to God, and various ways to order them by law, but they do not depend on church or state for their existence or for their meaning to the people who share them.

Marginal Christianity learns to build on that shared experience rather than wait for legal authorization or withdraw into the security of a confessional community. It gets things done rather than waits for authorization. It prefers to ask for forgiveness, rather than permission, to quote a favorite strategic axiom of the marginalized. It helps people accomplish what they seek rather than demands the enactment of its own program. Only later do those who have been helped find that their own expectations have been transformed, and the whole order of social possibilities has been altered.

All of this is unsatisfactory, theologically and politically, to those whose politics is still framed in Reformation terms. Those whose politics is descended, however remotely, from Luther's separation of secular authority and sacramental community get nervous when people start talking about secular action in terms of their Christian vocation. The secular-minded often approve of the results, but they find the method difficult to square with their expectation that if people can agree on what they want, they ought not to risk that consensus by using too much religious language to say why they want it. The radically separate Christian witness, by contrast, seems to be perplexed or angered by the strategic successes of marginal Christianity. Living the faith within society is not supposed to work, for theological reasons. So if it appears to work, the most likely explanation is that someone has been unfaithful, and what matters is faithfulness, not effectiveness.

Bishop Willimon has warned us against the dangers of proclaiming a gospel that depends too much on worldly successes.[20] The good news of salvation, he insists, is not a compendium of good advice about family relations, financial success, or positive thinking about ourselves and our situation. He is quite right, of course, about the importance of preserving the integrity of the gospel, but we must be careful not to confuse integrity with separation. A gospel that is about incarnation cannot draw too sharp a line between sacred and secular, between what is truly divine and what is merely human.

If you set the problem of church and society in the Reformation-era terms that still dominate much of Protestant thinking at the beginning of the twenty-first century, if there is only secular authority or spiritual, only politics or faith, then the Christian choice will lie with faith, and politics will be at best a kind of disagreeable service undertaken on behalf of one's neighbors. But if there is a politics of the workplace and of the school and of the museum, alongside the politics of church and state, if there is, in short, a kind of politics for every vocation that people share, then it seems to me that it is very much a part of the Christian vocation to make these things work. Our goal is to be both faithful and effective. Wesleyan Christians insist that effectiveness in creating shared human goods is a witness to our faith. Wesleyan Christians insist that the tragic choice between faithfulness and effectiveness is itself a sign of structural evils that must be addressed and, if possible, overcome. To accept the choice between faithfulness and effectiveness as a given is to deny our vocation.

To serve the present age and fulfill our calling, we must join with others, wherever we find ourselves, to create the conditions under which we can experience what human dignity means. Only then can our governments and our international institutions formulate declarations of human rights that will be effective in human life. And if we accept that calling and fulfill it, this will not just be a service to our neighbors but a working out of our own salvation. It will not be just an application of the gospel of Jesus Christ to a separate, secular reality but a way of understanding how the love of God fills all things and reaches every person.

CHAPTER EIGHT

"THE WORLD IS MY PARISH" —IS IT? WESLEYAN ECCLESIO-MISSIOLOGICAL CONSIDERATIONS FROM A CONTEMPORARY LATIN AMERICAN PERSPECTIVE

Paulo Ayres Mattos

What mystery is this! . . . Is not scriptural Christianity preached and generally known among the people commonly called Methodists? . . . Why is not the spiritual health of the people called Methodists recovered? . . . Why has Christianity done so little good, even among us? . . . Plainly because we have forgot, or at least not duly attended to those solemn words of our Lord, "If any man will come after me, let him deny himself, and take up his cross daily and follow me." . . . But why is self-denial in general so little practised at present among the Methodists? Why is so exceeding little of it to be found even in the oldest and largest societies? . . . The Methodists grow more and more self-indulgent, because they grow rich. . . . But how astonishing a thing is this! How can we understand it? Does it not seem (and yet this cannot be!) that Christianity, true scriptural Christianity, has a tendency in process of time to undermine and destroy itself? . . . Riches naturally beget pride, love of the world, and every temper that is destructive of Christianity.[1]

As Wesley neared death, Methodism had become sick. In this sermon of 1789 Wesley recognized that after five decades of revival it was not holiness, "inward and outward in all its forms," that had spread over the land, but the sickness of "wickedness of every kind." As in Wesley's latter days, it seems to me that Methodism today is sick in many parts of Latin America, as it may be elsewhere.

A problematic theological issue for Latin American Methodism is a weak ecclesiology. I would therefore like to explore, from a Latin American perspective, within the context of changes in North American Methodism that have affected Latin American churches, the following missiological affirmations of John Wesley: "I look upon the world as my parish,"[2] and "you have nothing to do but to save souls."[3] These affirmations will guide us as we seek theological criteria for an ecclesiological reorientation that may help our Latin American churches overcome our corporate weaknesses, and, at same time, reaffirm our missiological calling "to reform the nation, particularly the Church, and spread scriptural holiness over the land."[4]

IS THERE A WESLEYAN ECCLESIOLOGY?

Raised more than four decades ago, Outler's question, "Do Methodists have a doctrine of the church?"[5] is still a controversial issue in the field of Methodist studies. David Carter has pointed out that this is not a new question for Methodism, particularly for British Methodism, due to its genetic *vinculum* with the Church of England.[6] North American Methodism is another story. The lack of interest in ecclesiological themes among North American Methodist theologians during the nineteenth century is one of the striking consequences of the changes the new church experienced.[7] In the twentieth century as well, not much attention has been given to the theme in mainline North American Methodism.[8]

One of the most crucial problems faced by ecclesiological studies among Methodist scholars today is the subordination of the doctrine of the church to the doctrine of mission, that is, mission as the key for the church's self-understanding, as illustrated by the maxim "church is mission." Kissack affirms that "Methodism has traditionally been less concerned with what the Church is, than what it is for, and has found no activity more important than soliciting the right response of faith to the preaching of the gospel. The word 'sent' has more significance for the Church's understanding of itself than the word 'is.'"[9] Much has been said about the missional understanding of Methodist ecclesiology, according to Outler, and later Baker, as functional. This rationale often goes back to Outler's argument that Methodists are much more concerned with church *in actum* than with church *per se*.[10]

In light of the tendency that Kissack has rightly articulated, Bryan Stone makes a somewhat surprising statement from a Latin American perspective:

> The ecclesiology that currently underwrites the contemporary practice of evangelism—at least that which predominates in North America—is at best an ecclesiology where the church is either instrumentalized in the service of "reaching" or "winning" non-Christians, or a reduction of the church to a mere aggregate of autonomous believers, the group terminus of individual Christian converts. *Such an ecclesiology derives from an alternative social imagination made possible by modern, liberal philosophical and capitalist economic assumptions about history and about the nature of the self and its agency in the world. . . .* The Church becomes a whole that is actually less than a sum of its isolated, autonomous parts, each of which is busy pursuing its own private self-interests (including "getting saved").[11] [emphasis mine]

Furthermore, reacting to the notion that in Methodism church was derived from mission, which makes mission a central and crucial mark of the church, Stone makes a sharp comment:

> Especially in North America, missional ends are . . . developed as if the salvific social creation called "church" does not really matter. Mission becomes the central and crucial mark of the church rather than ecclesiality being the central and crucial mark of mission. It is then a simple step to disembody mission, separating it from the worship, practices, disciplines, and saintly lives—in short, "the body"—that constitute the church as God's holy new creation. From this development, I think, Wesleyans in North America have never quite recovered.[12]

With Stone's methodological approach, in which missiology depends on ecclesiology and ecclesiology on soteriology, we will surely reach different conclusions about the relations between Wesley's soteriology, ecclesiology, and missiology.[13]

WESLEY'S ECCLESIOLOGY

Wesley's ecclesiology is defined sometimes as Anglo-Catholic, other times as classical Reformed, and yet again as radical Protestant. Without ignoring the importance of such contributions to the discussion of Methodist ecclesiology, I would like to take another entry point for this discussion, trying to explore a different trajectory at the center of Wesley's theology and practice: Christian life as *via salutis*. Wesleyan theology in Brazil, particularly the work of Rui Josgrilberg, prioritizes this soteriological emphasis in Wesley's theology.[14]

Wesley's irregularities, particularly after 1738, were justified not only by pragmatic and functional reasons raised out of the missionary-evangelistic demands faced by the Methodist revival[15] but also by other theological opinions and pastoral experiences that came to influence Wesley's thought and practice over those years. By the late 1740s, in the context of his "irregularities," Wesley had gone through some crucial theological reinterpretations of the doctrine of the church in his pastoral and evangelistic practices, and more "lawful or unlawful" actions were in store for the Methodist movement in the next four decades. Willingly or not, Wesley developed throughout his life an ecclesiology that much of today's Methodist scholarship recognizes as a complex balance between the Anglo-Catholic understanding of the church and Moravian-Pietist traditions.[16]

It seems to me that this insight is crucial for a more accurate understanding of Wesley's ecclesiology, a corrective to its "functional" understanding. To define Wesley's ecclesiological developments as functional is, in my opinion, to downplay the critical balance between his soteriological and sacramental views of the church. Wesley's theology and practice were primarily centered in his soteriology. If soteriology, as "the scriptural way of salvation" more than "the order of salvation," was the pivotal element in Wesley's preaching and teaching, then to characterize his ecclesiology as functional says too little. I would prefer to characterize it as soteriological ecclesiology. Wesley understood salvation as "the entire work of God, *from* the first dawning of grace in the soul, *till* it is consummated in glory."[17] Furthermore, Maddox insists that Wesley was much more than a pragmatic evangelist.[18] Wesley was a practical theologian, pastor, and evangelist who kept theology and pastoral work in relational interconnectedness.[19]

Another soteriological axis present in Wesley's work was the church as a means of grace. It is in the context of the Church of England that the Methodist revival and its societies promoted and developed its soteriological work. Wesley believed that the original design of the church of Christ was "a body of men compacted together, in order, first, to save each his own soul; and then to assist each other in working out their salvation: and, afterwards, as far as in them lies, to save all men from present and future misery, to overturn the kingdom of Satan, and set up the kingdom of Christ."[20] Henry H. Knight reminds us that Wesley did not consider being a faithful member of the Church of England and at the same time a committed participant in the Methodist society at all contradictory. Because the Church of England was presupposed to be the context for Wesley's Methodist societies, he "saw the means of grace associated to the church as complementary to those of the societies, and as themselves necessary to the Christian life."[21] Thus "Wesley had no reservations about encouraging his people to seek God's grace through the various outward signs, words, and actions that God has ordained as 'ordinary' channels for conveying saving grace to humanity."[22]

It is with this soteriological perspective that we must understand the famous emblematic directives of early Methodism: "You have nothing to do but to save souls," "I look upon the world as my parish," and "to reform the nation, particularly the Church, and spread scriptural holiness over the land." These directives constituted an intrinsic and indivisible unity of Wesley's practical divinity between soteriology, ecclesiology, and missiology.

THE HISTORICAL RELATIONSHIP BETWEEN LATIN AMERICAN AND NORTH AMERICAN METHODISMS

After an initial unsuccessful attempt to bring Methodism to Argentina, Brazil, and Uruguay in the 1830s, Methodist missions were established and consolidated in several Latin American countries by both northern and southern Methodist churches in the second half of the nineteenth century. After so many decades of work, mainline Methodism in many parts of Latin America is yet weak. This observation does not ignore, much less deny, the transformations that thousands of people have experienced in their lives through the work of Methodism. However, many of our Methodist churches in today's Latin America live through serious instabilities and deficiencies in their praxis as God's people. Within the recent globalized capitalistic context, under neoliberal market economy, surrounded by all sorts of postmodern "evangelical" extravaganzas, many of our local congregations and their pastors have succumbed to a new spiritual idolatry of "novelties," as Wesley surely would describe such events. Many of our churches exist largely in a grave crisis in their Methodist identity.

Latin American Methodism cannot be understood without taking into consideration its North American origins. Therefore, the study of the historical developments of early North American Methodism that shaped its ecclesiological doctrine is fundamental for the understanding of the Methodism that was carried to Latin America by the missionaries of both Methodist Episcopal Churches, especially in the late-nineteenth century and early-twentieth century.

I will now explore from a Latin American perspective some ecclesio-missiological considerations related to crucial alterations in North American Methodism. The following considerations are not intended to be a judgment of good or bad, right or wrong, purity or impurity, but are offered as an understanding of continuities in discontinuities and also of discontinuities in continuities in these mutations. The intention of this approach is the development of a theological critique that may help us understand the sources of an ecclesiological weakness in those churches established by the missionary enterprise in Latin America of both Methodist Episcopal

Churches during the second half of the nineteenth century and the first decades of the last century. I am aware that this kind of approach may fall easily into what Russell Richey has identified as a jeremiadic historical reading of North American Methodism.[23] However, in light of Richey's argument, my intention is not to deploy criticism as a strategy of coping with our scarce membership growth or with the continuing feuds in some of our churches. Nor do I want to employ any uncritical positivistic reading of and claim to Wesley's teachings to cure our present ecclesiological troubles in Latin America. But neither do I want to ignore their historical mutated mediations in and by North American Methodism.

The first Methodist preachers appointed by Wesley arrived in America as representatives of a renewal movement within the established Church of England, in connection with and under the supervision of earnest Tory churchmen. They arrived in North America a few years before the independence of the thirteen colonies. Their task was to support the early North American Methodism established by migrant lay people outside Wesley's connection in Great Britain. The North American context, however, was quite different from eighteenth-century England. In fact, America at that time was on the periphery of a colonial power. On the one side of the Atlantic, a new industrial and urban society was being engendered in the womb of British power; on the other, the rural and agrarian periphery as the source of raw materials for the imperial center struggled against the exploitation imposed by the metropolis. Preachers sent by Wesley were very early confronted by a political revolution that did not believe in divine royal rights and proclaimed that all people had the right to political and religious freedom. John Wesley's Methodism and revolution were at odds. However, a few years later, in 1784, in order to assure that in the new country Methodists could preserve their soteriological design, Wesley felt that there was a necessity to form an independent Methodist connection in America, albeit still under his supervision but "at full liberty simply to follow the Scriptures and the primitive church." In order to assure full spiritual assistance to Methodist people in America, Wesley considered his providences the "more rational and scriptural way of feeding and guiding those poor sheep in the wilderness."[24] But his first concern above all in the formation of a church was to provide an order that could assure believers' access to the instituted means of grace.

The new religious world remained in its labor pangs for some decades. The Great Awakening that swept New England not only created a new religious mood unknown before, but, with the cooperation of George Whitefield's irregularities,[25] had challenged the established religious monopolies in the colonies. Market economy development was the context for the construction of a North American religious setting in which free enterprise and competition shaped the constitutional separation between church and state and the rise of the American Protestant denominations, a different sort of religious voluntary society.

The experimental reinventions of Wesleyan theology took place within a process that Thomas Langford has defined as the "Americanization of Wesleyan theology."[26] North American Methodists had to reinvent their soteriology, particularly Wesley's understanding of the fundamental place and role of the poor in the sanctification process;[27] reinvent their ecclesiology, in particular the practice of the different Wesleyan expressions of Christian conference as means of grace; and reinvent the nature of their missiology, changing the original Wesleyan design for Methodist preachers, not "to form any new sect; but to reform the nation, particularly the Church; and to spread scriptural holiness over the land."

In my opinion, Wesley's soteriology was deeply changed by the early controversy over slavery immediately after the Christmas conference. Soon the struggle against American slavery, "the vilest that ever saw the sun,"[28] became, gradually but persistently, a political affair subordinated to planters' economic interests, instead of an article of holiness of heart and life. The soteriological presence of the poorest among the poor in North American Methodist ecclesiology and spirituality was left behind, and discrimination and later segregation were theologically and ecclesiastically sanctioned.[29]

Notwithstanding, British Methodist preachers appointed by Wesley to North America strongly witnessed to the Methodists' deep aversion to the sin of slavery. Russell Richey reminds us that "freedom from sin and freedom from slavery belonged together, so early Methodists thought."[30] In the organization of the Methodist

Episcopal Church, American Methodists followed faithfully Wesley's admonition regarding the exercise of their full liberty. Under the leadership of Thomas Coke and Francis Asbury, the 1784 Christmas Conference once again openly reiterated Methodist opposition to slavery. Yet, when the Methodist founding fathers determined that all Methodists who owned slaves between the ages of forty and forty-five should emancipate them in twelve months, they also opened an exception to their strongly worded opposition. The rule would be applied only when the law of the states in which Methodists lived allowed such emancipation. The whole issue of slavery was going to receive a reinterpretation quite different from that understood in Wesley's General Rules. Within the political framework of the North American capitalist society, "the cost of antislavery proved high, too high for Methodism to sustain. But the cost of giving up proved high as well."[31]

In 1780 Asbury considered "purity, as he defined it, . . . far more important than unity—an admirable sentiment—as purity for Asbury at this time included both sacramental and social purity, but four years later Asbury was of opinion that unity was more important than the loss of purity that attended slaveholding."[32] For the next three decades a soteriological necessity would yield more and more to a very controversial political expedient, within and outside the Methodist camp; freedom from slavery became more and more a "spiritual" matter and institutional slavery was viewed as an economic necessity. General and annual conferences sometimes had fierce confrontations on the issue of slavery, but several of them were quite silent on it. The 1792 Conference deleted the expression "of the bodies and souls" from the *Discipline* that restricted "the buying or selling of the bodies and souls of men, women, or children, with an intention to enslave them."[33] Thus salvation of the soul was to become the core of North American Methodist soteriology. Amelioration instead of emancipation was accommodation to worldly standards—to the slaveholder's world.[34]

In the decades following Asbury's death, the change in the understanding of slavery among North American Methodists was motivated by their increasing concern for growth and organization.[35] However, church growth, understood as increasing membership numbers, was not a major priority in the very beginning of the Methodist Episcopal Church—holiness was. Despite facing internal and external troubles for their antislavery witness, Coke and Asbury in their introduction to the 1796 Minutes of the General Conference of the Methodist Episcopal Church would still dare to affirm, "Our grand object is to raise and preserve a holy and united people. Holiness is our aim; and we pay no regard to numbers, but in proportion as they possess the genuine principles of vital religion."[36] Political pressures against Methodist antislavery preaching increasingly became an obstacle to Methodist evangelistic work, including among the slaves. In the retreat to a more introverted understanding of Christian salvation, "Methodism lost something of itself. . . . For Methodists, as for many religious movements, growth and development may look like progress and success from some angles but appear retrogressive and ambiguous from others."[37]

The strong argument in favor of a more cautious and moderate attitude toward slavery accompanied the unquestionable church growth of North American Methodism in the following years.[38] The increasing membership of the Methodist Episcopal Church manifested God's approval of Methodist preaching and practices. Donald Matthews calls our attention to this point when he states,

> The great success of Methodist preaching was interpreted as the result of Divine pleasure. Excited evangelical oratory, emotional ecstasy, and the constant organization of new societies swept converts into the new Zion at such a speed that it grew from 15,000 members in 1784 to 58,000 in 1790. Confronted with such spectacular results, many preachers might have turned away from enthusiasm for emancipation and contented themselves with religious instruction of the slaves.[39]

Thus Methodist soteriology in North America was to suffer deep change in its content and form, particularly as regards the Wesleyan doctrine of entire sanctification in its close and inseparable connection with works of mercy and works of piety. This process was influenced by the social and economic transformations experienced within North American society and ended by focusing on individual soteriology, thus disregarding the church's teaching.[40] In face of such theology, ministry with the poor as a soteriological mark of the church lost its theological relevance.

Now we turn to an ecclesiological issue in order to clarify matters. North American Methodism in its early stage in the late eighteenth century reproduced Wesley's social religion of societies, classes, and bands as prudential means of grace and as an intrinsic part of his soteriology and ecclesiology.[41]

Wesley is clear on this point of social religion when he says, "By Christianity I mean that method of worshipping God which is here revealed to man by Jesus Christ. When I say, this is essentially a social religion, I mean not only that it cannot subsist so well, but that it cannot subsist at all, without society, without living and conversing with other men."[42] Thus, reflecting on the character of the social religion in the process of the growth in holiness of heart and life, Wesley affirms that in order that "his followers may the more effectually provoke one another to love, holy tempers, and good works, our blessed Lord has united them together in one body, the Church, dispersed all over the earth; a little emblem of which, of the Church universal, we have in every particular Christian congregation."[43] Wesley's revival was built on the necessity for social religion.[44] Christian experience can take place not in solitary encounter with God but only in the relational context of Christian community.

The emphasis of ecclesiology on social religion, however, later suffered a deep alteration when Christian conference as a means of grace became, gradually but persistently, merely a meeting that focused on church polity and business, while revival was engulfed by camp-meeting, and sanctification turned into subjective and individualist experiences. Richey has noted that in North American Methodism "when revivalism became an end in itself, an interiorization and individualization of religion resulted . . . as Methodism found its place in American society."[45] However, Richey recognizes that while early Methodist revivalism was indisputably individualistic, it is nevertheless possible to portray it "as a communal affair."[46]

As the Church prospered numerically, financially, and institutionally, the spiritual aspect of conference gave way to business and legislation. The Methodist response for the split between conference and revival was, in Richey's view, the "miracle" of camp meeting.[47] Camp meeting with its individualism, and its instantaneous and emotional message of salvation, radically changed the corporate nature of the Wesleyan Christian conference. As a consequence, Methodist soteriology increasingly lost its social character and the balanced tension between social and personal holiness, between the works of piety and works of mercy in their interconnectedness, so characteristic of Wesley's social religion.

North American Methodist soteriological holiness became more and more a private and domestic affair.[48] It became an intimate and introverted experience motivated by and lived in camp meeting revivals and nourished in Methodist chapels and homes, and over the years, less and less at class meetings. A unilateral emphasis on the subjective works of piety displaced works of mercy and tended to obscure the nature of "the church as a means of grace."[49] In its multiple diversity, from the bottom to the top of the "Methodist machinery," from class meeting to General Conference, Wesley's Christian conference lost its ecclesiological dimension as a means of grace. According to Maddox, this began "the eclipse of the Church as a means of grace in American Methodism."[50]

Such ecclesiological mutation was also expressed in North American Methodist reinterpretation of God's design for Methodism on this continent, evidenced by a deep change in the original Methodist missional self-understanding. Twenty-five years after Aldersgate, when John Wesley in 1763 faced the well-known question, "What may we reasonably believe to be God's design, in raising up the Preachers called Methodists?" his reply was "To reform the nation, and, in particular, the Church; to spread scriptural holiness over the land."[51] The evangelical revival was a spiritual response to England's national and ecclesial crisis. At stake was the evangelical missional calling vis-à-vis corruption in nation and church. Wesley's concern for the salvation of his soul and the souls of others made clear that not only the nation should be reformed but, in particular, the church. The soteriological importance of the church as a means of grace made its reformation an urgent necessity. Wesley's perception of Methodism's urgent missional calling derived from his soteriological ecclesiology: doing defined by being, being expressed by doing.

The Christmas Conference in 1784, reflecting a different self-understanding in response to a different historical-missiological context, affirmed that God's design in raising up Methodist preachers in North America was "to reform the continent, and to spread scriptural holiness over these lands."[52] "Continent" instead of Wesley's "nation," no more reference to "the church," and the singular "land" replaced by the plural "lands."

The United States of America was a new nation trying to establish and consolidate its political institutions and capitalist economic structures, of which slavery was one of the foundations. It is clear that the Methodist Episcopal Church, in such economic and political context, had to show full loyalty to the new nation, to its regimen and government, especially after many Methodists had refused to take the prescribed oath of allegiance during the Revolution.[53] But they did this in a very subtle way, substituting "the continent" for Wesley's "nation, and particularly the Church."

The separation between church and state, as it was established in the new nation of the United States of America, did not eliminate the deep structural relationship and interconnectedness between religion and society. Since the very beginning of Methodism's institutional life as an independent denomination, North American Methodists could not avoid theological and practical adjustments, the religious accommodations that would respond to concrete economic, political, and social needs of the new country. Therefore, even when Methodists in North America were aware of national sins such as slavery, an economic and social structure so fundamental for the development of the agrarian and industrial North America, they pretended to maintain distance from such worldly evils. They erected strict boundaries between the Methodist family and the "world." The new church did not understand that God's design for them necessarily implied national reformation as Wesley had discerned for his own England. The American continent was their missional locus, not the North American nation. Not just the "land," but the "lands," much land, to be conquered, explored, and, surely, exploited.[54]

Such missional understanding of Asbury and other early Methodist Episcopal leaders in North America about "the continent" reproduced the common ideology of *terra nulla* (empty land) of most colonizers since Columbus[55] invaded the "lands" that came to be known as Americas. Missing in these descriptions are the peoples of "the lands," the Native Americans. When Richey mentions the firsthand experience of the Methodist itinerant preachers vis-à-vis the challenges of the continent, the words he uses have to do mostly with geography, not people: rivers, mountains, swamps, thickets, forests, downpours, snowfalls, and mosquitoes, the "wilderness" of the first colonizers! What about the first dwellers of those lands? Furthermore, in Asbury's *Journal* and *Letters* the references to Native Americans are almost always in very negative terms, as dangerous, cruel, and barbaric peoples. It is true that on different occasions Asbury manifested his concern about the evangelization of the Native Americans, trying to follow Wesley's strong recommendations in his 1787 letter on the neglected evangelization of the Indian nations in North and South America.[56] However, only in 1815, twenty-eight years after Wesley's letter and one year before Asbury's death, was the Methodist work among Native Americans unofficially initiated when an irregular preacher established a mission to the Wyandot Indians in Ohio. This was the beginning of official missionary work.[57]

The understanding of the continent as *terra nulla* led North American Methodism to reinforce and deepen its theological and practical schizophrenia already implied in its compromises with slavery interests and in the alterations that broke continuity with Wesley's social religion as means of grace. In that sense, Methodism in North America renounced Wesley's concern for the reformation of nation, as well of church, as part of holy living on the way of salvation. It thereby lost touch with Wesley's soteriological ecclesiology and missiology. According to Richey, the church adopted a "political passivity that made Methodists relatively uninterested in the nature and the meaning of the American political experiment." North American Methodists ended up adjusting their theology and missionary practices to hegemonic capitalist political and economic interests that have shaped in many ways North American social and religious structures: (1) soteriological "free grace" was reduced to anthropological "gracious ability," and later to "free will"; (2) Wesley's social religion was changed to intimate, subjective, emotional, individualistic experience, in which church became merely an instrument for the salvation of individuals; (3) the mutual accountability of the Christian conference, social and personal, across varying Methodist expressions of Christian conversations, from the inner circle of class meetings to annual preachers' conferences, dissipated in the midst of the massive camp meetings and in the business and politics of the annual conferences; (4) works of mercy, as expressions of Jesus' option for the poor, lost their soteriological nature when turned into charitable "works of benevolence"; (5) "nation," as a concrete reality, with its corporate virtues and sins, the result of human experiments, an arena in which the divine and the demonic reflected the ways people respond to God's love and grace, was turned into an ambiguous "continent," the empty land to be conquered, subjected to the naturalization of politics and socioeconomic relationships; and (6) evangelization was reduced to numeric church growth and middle-class respectability.

These transformations led decades later to the need many Methodists in North America felt, on one side, for a national movement that promoted scriptural holiness, and, on the other, for a movement that upheld a social gospel. Within Wesley's practical divinity, it seems to me, both movements would be inconceivable, inappropriate, a negation of the holiness of heart and life. The General Rules offered to the Methodist people on the way of salvation the provisions for their growth in holy living. Love of neighbor (expressed in the works of mercy) and love of God (expressed in the works of piety) could not ever be separated in the process of working out their salvation. The results of such mutations may be observed in the increasingly divisive processes that characterized North American Methodism throughout the nineteenth century.

Unfortunately, when Methodist missions arrived in Latin America, during the second half of the nineteenth century and in the first decades of the twentieth century, they arrived already divided into several Methodist denominations and by different theologies and practices. Within such a missionary context, it is not hard to understand the present ecclesiological and missiological difficulties that those different expressions of Methodism face in today's Latin America.

Methodist Churches in Latin America

The changes within North American Methodism created instabilities and deficiencies in its soteriology, ecclesiology, and missiology that even today deeply affect the life and mission of the Methodist churches in Latin America. In Latin America the continuous breeding of the struggles and conflicts between liberals and conservatives, between traditionalists and charismatics, between ecumenists and anti-ecumenists, between mainline Methodists and Holiness Methodists, between Methodists in general and Pentecostals, come in part from these nineteenth-century North American alterations. These conflicts centered in particular on the issues of freedom for African slaves, the poorest among the poor, on the issue of Christian conference as means of grace, and on the understanding of God's design for the people called Methodists in these lands.

It is true that during the last thirty years or so, significant endeavors have emerged for working to overcome this "crisis of identity," and God's spirit has not abandoned our Methodist people in Latin America. Under inspiration of the ecumenical theology of the *missio Dei*, some of our churches have decided to begin the process of renewal motivated by and in accordance with the Wesleyan roots of early Methodism, particularly in its mandate to "spread scriptural holiness over the land."

In this process, the rediscovering of Wesley's affirmations about his understanding of the way of salvation in its intrinsic soteriological connection, between personal and social holiness, became a crucial factor for a renewed emphasis on the Wesleyan teaching on sanctification. Many Latin American Methodists have affirmed again and again, with Wesley, that true Christianity cannot exist without both the inward experience of personal holiness and the outward practice of the justice, mercy, and truth of social holiness, not because of some ideological option but because it is a soteriological article for Methodists. Again with Wesley we can affirm, "The gospel of Christ knows of no religion, but social; no holiness but social holiness."

Despite the persistent presence of an individualistic salvation and inward holiness in the life of many Methodist local churches in Latin America, a spirituality that emphasizes "one-sided spiritualized introverted" practices, the renewal efforts have created many new missionary possibilities for Methodist commitment to the spiritual needs of our peoples. The Wesleyan teaching on "holiness of heart and life" has found increasingly greater expressions in different forms of personal and social witnesses, through concrete responses to diverse evils present in our societies.

We must acknowledge, however, that the "crisis of identity" that has been affecting Latin American Methodism in the last four decades or so is not over and is being experienced also by other mainline denominations, including the Roman Catholic Church and the well-established classical Pentecostal churches. Furthermore, in the last two decades the tremendous growth and influence of the new Pentecostal churches—established in response to postmodern religious demands, with very little connection with Protestant-evangelical theology, or even with classical Pentecostal theology—are new factors that have brought crises to those denominations.

If the heart of John Wesley's theology is salvation, then the ecclesial marks of a Wesleyan ecclesiology must be soteriological marks. Albert Outler years ago affirmed,

> The Church is *one* in the Spirit rather than in any of its institutional structures; it is *holy* in the Spirit, who calls and leads the faithful into that holy living without which none shall see the Lord. It is *catholic*, both in terms of Wesley's "catholic spirit" and in its radical commitment to actual inclusiveness; it is *apostolic* in the Spirit, who once turned a dispirited rabble into a company of witnesses and servants, and can work this same miracle again—as the Spirit has so often in the history of the Christian community.[58]

Therefore, it seems to me that Latin American Methodists, in order "to serve the present age, [their] calling to fulfill," should not try to restore or imitate early Methodism—that would be quite impossible. Our worlds are completely different; the needs, the desires, the possibilities, the limitations are deeply distinct. However, by reappropriating the Wesleyan theological legacy in our context, we can try to be obedient to God's gracious work, as John Wesley and early Methodists did in their own age. Above all, it is necessary to appropriate again and again the centrality of God's reign for our soteriology, ecclesiology, and missiology, actualizing in our ecclesial context Wesley's commitment "to save all people from present and future misery, to overturn the kingdom of Satan, and set up the kingdom of Christ." Under such spiritual commitment, it seems to me that we Latin American Methodist churches should do the following: (1) Reappropriate Wesley's charge, "you have nothing to do but to save souls," and develop strong ecclesiological concern for an all-inclusive soteriology, a soteriology in which solidarity *with* the poor, not *for* the poor, must be a soteriological article of faith instead of an ideological option, regardless of resistance by the unjust and oppressive economic and political demands of the present powers.[59] (2) Reappropriate Wesley's affirmation, "I look upon the world as my parish," and develop a strong ecclesiological concern for a spirituality in which, within this world, all God's people may be accountable to the personal and social means of grace on our way to holiness of heart and life, working out our salvation through the disciplined exercise of the works of mercy and piety in the midst of daily life. (3) Reappropriate as a strong ecclesiological concern Wesley's charge "to reform the nation, particularly the Church, and spread scriptural holiness over the land." This would mean assuming as a soteriological article the challenge to the powers in church and society and overcoming all prejudice, in particular against the most vulnerable people in our midst. Thus, with Wesley, we will be able to proclaim, "So that the salvation which is here spoken of might be extended to the entire work of God, from the first dawning of grace in the soul, till it is consummated in glory."

In face of the tremendous missionary challenges posed by the present Latin American social, political, cultural, and religious contexts to the rather small Methodist churches, I believe that the time has come for us to assert that our major priority should be reappropriating in our historical contexts the original message of early Methodism on the centrality of the church as means of grace. This requires strong spiritual accountability of Christian discipleship in daily life, based on a radical obedience to God's calling for holy living for all creation, through disciplined works of piety and works of mercy, in personal and social holiness of heart and life.

The author expresses his gratitude to Mark C. Shenise, the Associate Archivist of The United Methodist Church (General Commission on Archives and History—Madison, N.J., USA), for his gracious assistance in the preparation of this essay.

NOTES

2. What If Wesley Was Right?

1. My teacher Lee Keck got me thinking about the Oxford Institute in this way with his essay, "What If Paul Was Right?" in Christine Roy Yoder, Cathleen M. O'Connor, E. Elizabeth Johnson, and Stanley P. Saunders, eds., *Shaking Heaven and Earth: Essays in Honor of Walter Brueggemann and Charles B. Cousar* (Louisville: Westminster/John Knox, 2005), 133–39.
2. "Advice to Preachers, August 1, 1786," *Minutes*, 193–94.
3. See the 1744 sermon of that title.
4. Bishop Scott Jones lists "the ten essential doctrines" that tie Wesleyans together in very deep ways: Trinity, including Christology; Creation; Sin; Repentance; Justification; New Birth; Assurance; Sanctification; Grace; and Mission. While Jones's list is helpful, I think such essentialism is not the most fruitful way to listen to Wesley. Better to discern the impulse for and direction of his spiritual pilgrimage that encouraged him to join with fellow pilgrims in embodiment of the *imitatio Christi* in allowing God to transform God's world and their own lives.
5. "Nothing is so small or insignificant in the sight of men as not to be an object of the care and providence of God, before whom nothing is small that concerns the happiness of any of his creatures."
6. *Letters*, 25:257–58.
7. John 16:24, "Ask, and ye shall receive, that your joy may be full." *Hymns and Sacred Poems* (1739), 219–21.
8. Changed to "Mine I see, whate'er is his" in 4th ed. (1743) and 5th ed. (1756).
9. Karl Barth, *The Epistle to the Romans*, trans. Edwyn C. Hoskyns, 6th ed. (London: Oxford University Press, 1933), 332.
10. Richard P. Heitzenrater, *Wesley and the People Called Methodists* (Nashville: Abingdon Press, 1995), 296.
11. Sermon preached at St. Mary's, January 1, 1733 (*Sermons*, 1:401–14).
12. Heitzenrater, *Wesley and the People Called Methodists*, 1.
13. Lately I've become fascinated by the lively debate among Pauline scholars that is reframing the old justification vs. sanctification debate as it relates to Paul. Peter Stuhlmacher, for instance, has demonstrated that justification in Romans is not so much reclamation of the sinner in the individual's struggle with guilt, but the active compassion of God that transforms sinners and prepares them for active discipleship. Peter Stuhlmacher, *Revisiting Paul's Doctrine of Justification* (Downers Grove, Ill.: InterVarsity, 2001), 62. The old controversy between Catholics and Protestants, distinguishing between "imputed" righteousness

(related only to sinners) and the Catholic view of "effective" righteousness that transforms sinners, cannot be sustained by reference to Pauline texts, says Douglas Harnick. The Reformation was wrong to buy into a view of justification that excludes sanctification. See Douglas Harnick, *Paul among the Postliberals* (Grand Rapids: Brazos, 2003), 57. Of course such sentiments are music to the ears of Arminians.

14. Barbara Brown Taylor, *Leaving Church: A Memoir of Faith* (San Francisco: HarperOne, 2006).

15. Wesleyan Thomas Oden, in his *Pastoral Theology: Essentials of Ministry* (San Francisco: Harper & Row, 1983), 8, charges the contemporary mainline church with pastoral care that has become mere "antinomianism." "Antinomianism is the weird, wild, impulsive, unpredictable sleeping partner of much contemporary pastoral care. It mistakes the gospel for license, freedom for unchecked self-actualization, and health for native vitalism." Our once pushy sanctificationism has been tamed to be nothing more than therapy. We've lost interest in society and have climbed into the almighty, autonomous self. We're Wesleyans, and ministry ought to have a considerably larger view of what is possible under God—nothing less than "reform of church and spread of holiness throughout the land."

16. Twelve of the original forty-four sermons were a series on the Sermon on the Mount—now Sermons 21–33, *Works*, 1:466–698. See also his equation of Christ's law with the Sermon on the Mount in his "Letter to an Evangelical Layman" (20 Dec. 1751), §3, *Works*, 26:482.

3. Ecclesiology from the Perspective of Scripture in Wesleyan and Asian Contexts

1. Albert Outler, "Do Methodists Have a Doctrine of the Church?" in *The Doctrine of the Church*, ed. Dow Kirkpatrick (Nashville: Abingdon Press, 1964), reprinted in Thomas C. Oden and Leicester R. Longden, eds., *The Wesleyan Theological Heritage: Essays of Albert C. Outler* (Grand Rapids: Zondervan, 1991), 211–26.

2. See A. W. Harrison, *The Separation of Methodism from the Church of England* (London: Epworth, 1945), 60, 61, and John M. Haley and Leslie J. Francis, eds., *British Methodism: What Circuit Ministers Really Think* (Peterborough: Epworth, 2006), 1–19.

3. For the meaning of *glocalization*, see the following section.

4. See Thomas L. Friedman, *The Lexus and the Olive Tree* (New York: Farrar, Straus and Giroux, 1999), and *The World Is Flat: A Brief History of the Twenty-first Century* (New York: Picador, 2007), 420–26.

5. J. D. Collins and Dr. and Mrs. Moses White were the earliest missionaries of the MEM to serve in China.

6. George Piercy, a farmer and a local preacher of Pickling Methodist Church in Yorkshire, was the first British Methodist missionary to serve in China via Hong Kong. The Methodist Church in Hong Kong was started by Chinese Methodists from Guangzhou and Foshan who started class meetings and worship in Hong Kong in 1882.

7. Macao is 60 kilometers away from Hong Kong Island. It became a Portuguese colony in 1557 and returned to China in December 1999.
8. The Methodist churches in Hong Kong, Korea, Malaysia, Singapore, India, and the Philippines are growing. New Methodist churches are being developed in Cambodia and Vietnam.
9. In 1950, a Chinese Christian Three-Self Patriotic Movement (TSPM) was launched in Beijing with the strong support of the Communist government, which had successfully broken all Western ties to Chinese churches.
10. Many books have been published in English on the Cultural Revolution, e.g., Barbara Barnouin and Changgen Yu, *Ten Years of Turbulence: The Chinese Cultural Revolution* (New York: Kegan Paul International, 1993).
11. According to K. H. Ting (1984), "A Rationale for Three-Self" collected in *A Chinese Contribution to Ecumenical Theology: Selected Writings of Bishop K. H. Ting*, ed. Janice and Philip Wickeri (Geneva: WCC, 2002), 66, there were not more than 700,000 before 1949. However, it is difficult to count the number of Christians in contemporary China with reliable evidence. According to the report of the Amity Foundation and a study of Tony Lambert, the figure in 2006 is not less than 20 million. The figures do not include Catholics and those who worship in nonregistered house churches.
12. Paul Minear, *Images of the Church in the New Testament* (Philadelphia: Westminster, 1961).
13. Ibid., 11. For other studies related to a similar concern, see Rudolf Schnackenburg (1965), *The Church in the New Testament*, trans. W. J. O'Hara (London: Burns & Oates, 1981); R. J. McKelvey, *The New Temple: The Church in the New Testament* (Oxford: Oxford University Press, 1969); also Hieromonk Alexander Golitzin, "Scriptural Images of the Church: An Eastern Orthodox Reflection," in *One, Holy, Catholic and Apostolic: Ecumenical Reflections on the Church*, ed. Tamara Grdzelidze, Faith and Order Paper, no. 197 (Geneva: WCC, 2005), 255–66.
14. Minear, *Images*, 63.
15. Emil Brunner, *The Word and the World* (New York: Scribner's Sons, 1931), 108; see also Karl Barth, *Kirchliche Dogmatik*, vol. 4, no. 3 (1959), 1002.
16. Outler, *Wesleyan Heritage*, 219, emphasis his.
17. See Haley and Francis, *British Methodism*, 237.
18. *Minjung* is a Korean word, a combination of two Chinese characters: *min* and *jung*. Min may be translated as "people" and *jung* as "the mass." Thus, *minjung* means "the mass of the people" or just "the people." See discussion in Yong Bock Kim, ed., *Minjung Theology: People as the Subjects of History* (Singapore: CCA, The Commission on Theological Concerns; Maryknoll, N.Y.: Orbis, 1981), and David Suh, *The Korean Minjung in Christ* (Hong Kong: CCA, 1991).
19. I. Howard Marshall, "New Wine in Old Wine-Skins: V. The Biblical Use of the Word 'Ekklesia,'" *Expository Times* 84 (1973): 362, and Peter O'Brien, "Church," in *Dictionary of Paul and His Letters*, ed. Gerald F. Hawthorne and Ralph P. Martin (Leicester: InterVarsity Press, 1993), 123.
20. L. Coenen, "Church, Synagogue," in *The International Dictionary of New Testament Theology*, ed. Colin Brown (Exeter: Paternoster, 1975), 291.

21. Marshall, *Expository Times*, 350.
22. O'Brien, *Dictionary of Paul*, 124.
23. *Sunagoge* is used more frequently in Genesis-Numbers and the Prophets; see W. Schrage, *sunagoge* in *TDNT*, vol. 7 (1971), 798–841. He suggests that the frequent use of *sunagoge* for translating both words in the Pentateuch is probably due to the desire of the translators to link the contemporary Jewish synagogues with the "synagogue" that received the Law (802).
24. Rudolf Bultmann, *Theology of the New Testament* (London: SCM, 1952), 1:38, followed by many scholars, such as W. D. Davies and Dale Allison, *A Critical and Exegetical Commentary on the Gospel According to Saint Matthew*, vol. 2, *Commentary on Matthew VIII–XVIII*, ICC (Edinburgh: T&T Clark, 1991), 629.
25. *Ekklesia* occurred mostly in Pauline letters; the term "people of God" occurred as "his (God's) people" only once in Romans 1:1 (*laon autou*). For discussion of the use of *laos* in the New Testament, see below.
26. See Alan Richardson, *An Introduction to the Theology of the New Testament* (London: SCM, 1958), 287–88.
27. The experiences of Methodists in the early stage are similar to the situation of the relationship between Jews and Christians in the early church; see Morna Hooker, *Continuity and Discontinuity: Early Christianity in Its Jewish Setting* (London: Epworth, 1986), 11–12.
28. See Ted Campbell, *Methodist Doctrine: The Essentials* (Nashville: Abingdon Press, 1999), 20, 25, 64, 77, 116; and Haley and Francis, *British Methodism*, 20–22, 82.
29. See Richard P. Heitzenrater, *Wesley and the People Called Methodists* (Nashville: Abingdon Press, 1995).
30. See Russell E. Richey, "Introduction," in *Connectionalism: Ecclesiology, Mission and Identity*, ed. Russell E. Richey, Dennis Campbell, and William B. Lawrence (Nashville: Abingdon Press, 1997), 3–7.
31. See John Wesley's Sermon LXXV, "On Schism."
32. See Campbell, *Methodist Doctrine*, 68.
33. Minear, *Images*, 67–68.
34. See H. Bietenhard, *laos* in *The International Dictionary of New Testament Theology*, ed. Colin Brown (Exeter: Paternoster, 1971), 795–800, see especially 798.
35. See discussion in E. Käsemann, *The Wandering People of God: An Investigation of the Letter to the Hebrews*, trans. Roy A. Harrisville and Irving L. Sandberg (Minneapolis: Augsburg, 1957).
36. Bietenhard, *International Dictionary*, 799–80.
37. According to the calculation of the numbers of adherents of major religions in the world in 2000, the estimation of Christians was 32.3 million (including Catholics, Protestants, and Eastern Orthodox); Muslims, 19.2 million; and Hindus, 13.7 million.
38. **See Haley and Francis, *British Methodism*, 6.**
39. **See discussion in Richard Heitzenrater, ed., *The Poor and the People Called Methodists, 1729–1999* (Nashville: Kingswood Books, 2002).**
40. See Hodgson, *People's Century: From the Dawn of the Century to the Eve of the Millennium*, BBC television series, combined ed. (Godalming: Colour Library

Direct, 1998). Note, however, that the book is decidedly West-centered; the people's movement in the Philippines in 1986, three years earlier than the 1989 people's movement in the Eastern Bloc of Europe, brought down the long rule of the dictator Marcos (1965–86) but was not even mentioned in the book. The student movement, which became a widely influential people's movement in China (May-June 1989), had tremendous impact on the development of China and probably also of the Eastern Bloc but is mentioned in fewer than five lines (480).

41. David Kwang-sun Suh, "*Minjung* and Theology in Korea: A Biographical Sketch of an Asian Theological Consultation," in *Minjung Theology,* ed. Yong Bock Kim, 18.

42. See Christian Institute for the Study of Justice and Development, *Presence of Christ among Minjung: Introduction to the UIM in Korea* (Seoul: Christian Institute for the Study of Justice and Development, 1981); The Commission on Theological Concerns, CCA ed., *Towards the Sovereignty of the People* (Singapore: CTC-CCA, 1983); Po-ho Huang, *An Introduction to Gospel and Culture: A Theology Nourished in Culture* (in Chinese, Tainan: Yen Kwang, 1987), and *An Interpretation of the Confession of Taiwan Presbyterian Church: A Faith Rooted in the Native Soil* (in Chinese, Tainan: Yen Kwang, 1991).

43. W. D. Davies and Dale C. Allison, *A Critical and Exegetical Commentary on the Gospel According to Saint Matthew,* vol. 2, *Commentary on Matthew VIII–XVIII,* ICC (Edinburgh: T&T Clark, 1991), 629.

44. Ibid.

45. Minear admits that "too little theological attention has been given to this mode [exodus] of perceiving the character of the church." *Images,* 272, n. 10.

46. John Wesley (1754) does not discuss this phrase in his explanation of this verse (420), and in the extant sermons he had neither preached on this verse nor referred to it in the footnotes; see Frank Baker, ed., *The Works of John Wesley* (Nashville: Abingdon Press, 1987), 670. However, the KJV, RSV, and the 1899 version of the Catholic Bible (London: R. & T. Washbourne) all translate the phrase as "the church in the wilderness"; there is a footnote in the RSV to denote "church" or "congregation."

47. C. K. Barrett, *A Critical and Exegetical Commentary on the Acts of the Apostles,* ICC (Edinburgh: T&T Clark, 1994), 1:365.

48. See Bruce M. Metzger, *A Textual Commentary on the Greek New Testament* (London: UBS, 1971), 304–5.

49. C. K. Barrett, *A Critical and Exegetical Commentary on the Acts of the Apostles,* ICC (Edinburgh: T&T Clark, 1998), 2:lxxxviii.

50. Barrett, *Critical Commentary,* 1:337.

51. Ibid., 338–40.

52. Barrett, *Critical Commentary,* 2:lxxxviii.

53. Campbell, *Methodist Doctrine: The Essentials* (Nashville, Abingdon Press, 1999), 59f.

54. Ibid., 60.

55. Ibid., emphasis mine. Campbell mentions the case of William Wilberforce, who was encouraged by Wesley to continue the effort to end human slavery in British territories.

56. See my discussion in Lung-kwong Lo, "The Nature of the Issue of Ancestral Worship among Chinese Christians," *Studies in World Christianity* 9, no. 1 (2003): 30–42.

57. Minear, *Images,* 139–43.

58. Ibid., 145–48.

59. Ibid., 152–55.

60. For the variation of seventy and seventy-two, see John Nolland, *Word Biblical Commentary,* vol. 35b, *Luke 9:21–18:34* (Dallas: Word, 1993), 549–50.

61. Martin Hengel, *The Charismatic Leader and His Followers,* trans. James Greig (Edinburgh: T&T Clark, 1981), 81, n. 163.

62. In 6:67, "the twelve" is mentioned for the first time in John.

63. C. K. Barrett, *Luke the Historian in Recent Study* (London: Epworth, 1961), suggests that Luke–Acts offers us two pictures of the church, one consciously, which may not be an accurate picture of the church of the first few decades in its relationship with Jesus himself, and another unconsciously, which does reflect the church of his time (24–25).

64. Minear, *Images,* 146. Furthermore, he says, "This connection is explicitly recognized within the Gospels themselves." He quotes Matthew, chaps. 5–7; 10:24-25; 19:13-30; Luke 9:57-61; 14:26-33; John 8:12; 10:4-5; 13:24-26.

65. Hengel, *Charismatic Leader,* 72–73.

66. See ibid., 78–79.

67. Ibid., 73. Regarding the controversial relationship between the kingdom of God and the church, note as phrased by the famous statement by Loisy that "Jesus foretold the kingdom; and it was the church that came." Alfred Loisy, *The Gospel and the Church* (*L'Evangileet et L'Eglise*), trans. Christopher Home (London: Isbister & Co., 1903), 166.

68. Hengel, *Charismatic Leader,* 61–63, 71–72; also James D. G. Dunn, *Jesus' Call to Discipleship* (Cambridge: Cambridge University Press, 1992), 92.

69. See Dunn, *Jesus' Call,* regarding the corporate dimensions of discipleship (92–94).

70. Campbell, *Methodist Doctrine,* 65. See also the discussion of Dietrich Bonhoeffer, *Sanctorum Communio: A Dogmatic Inquiry into the Sociology of the Church,* 3rd ed., trans. R. George Smith (London: Collins, 1963), especially its emphasis on church as a community of being "with one another" and "being for one another" (126–36, especially 129).

71. See D. Bonhoeffer, *The Cost of Discipleship,* trans. R. H. Fuller (London: SCM, 1959), 79.

72. A quotation from the famous Chinese historian Qian Si-ma, "A Letter Sent to Ren On."

73. Bonhoeffer, *Cost of Discipleship,* 35.

74. James D. G. Dunn, *The Theology of Paul the Apostle* (Grand Rapids: Eerdmans, 1998), 550.

75. Ronald Y. K. Fung, "Body of Christ," in *Dictionary of Paul and His Letters,* ed. Gerald F. Hawthorne and Ralph P. Martin (Downers Grove, Ill.: InterVarsity Press, 1993), 81.

76. Dunn, *Jesus' Call,* 93.

77. Bonhoeffer, *Cost of Discipleship*, 223.
78. J. A. T. Robinson, *The Body: A Study in Pauline Theology* (London: SCM, 1952), 68.
79. Graham Ward, "Bodies: The Displaced Body of Jesus Christ," in *Radical Orthodoxy: A New Theology* (London: Routledge, 1999), 163–81.
80. John Webster, "The Visible Attests the Invisible," in *The Community of the Word: Toward an Evangelical Ecclesiology*, ed. Mark Husbands and Daniel Treier (Downers Grove, Ill.: InterVarsity Press, 2005), 96–113.
81. See also Bonhoeffer, *Cost of Discipleship*, 213.
82. See Minear, *Images*, 197.
83. Ibid., 133.
84. Leviticus 26:12; Exodus 29:45; Ezekiel 37:27; Jeremiah 31:1; Isaiah 52:11; Hosea 1:10; Isaiah 43:6.
85. See also Philippians 2:17; 4:18; Colossians 1:12.
86. R. J. McKelvey, *The New Temple: The Church in the New Testament* (Oxford: Oxford University Press, 1969), 92, 106–7.
87. In Ephesians 2:20, the foundation is the apostles and prophets.
88. James D. G. Dunn, *Jesus and the Spirit* (London: SCM, 1975), 295.
89. Scott J. Jones, *United Methodist Doctrine: The Extreme Center* (Nashville: Abingdon Press, 2002), criticized the lack of a developed relationship between the Holy Spirit and the means of grace, and noted that United Methodist ecclesiology would benefit from the further expansion of the doctrine of Holy Spirit. See 115–16.
90. See C. S. Song, *Jesus in the Power of Spirit* (Minneapolis: Augsburg Fortress, 1994), 5–7.
91. Outler, *Wesleyan Heritage*, 224.

4. Work on Earth and Rest in Heaven

1. White in Kenneth G. C. Newport and Ted A. Campbell, eds., *Charles Wesley: Life, Literature and Legacy* (London: Epworth, 2007), 515–31.
2. Richard P. Heitzenrater in ST Kimbrough, ed, *Charles Wesley: Poet and Theologian* (Nashville: Abingdon Press, 1992), 181–82.
3. White in Newport and Campbell, *Life, Literature and Legacy*, 526.
4. Lloyd in Newport and Campbell, *Life, Literature and Legacy*, 1–17.
5. Gareth Lloyd, *Charles Wesley and the Struggle for Methodist Identity* (New York: Oxford University Press, 2007), 79, and in his article in Newport and Campbell, *Life, Literature and Legacy*, 12.
6. Lloyd, *Charles Wesley and the Struggle for Methodist Identity*, 242.
7. Angela Shier-Jones, *A Work in Progress: Methodists Doing Theology* (London: SPCK, 2005), 268–72.
8. Armand Larive, *After Sunday: A Theology of Work* (New York, Continuum, 2004), 3.
9. Chilcote in Paul W. Chilcote, ed., *The Wesleyan Tradition: A Paradigm for Renewal* (Nashville: Abingdon Press, 2002), 34.
10. *The Works of John Wesley*, Bicentennial Edition (hereafter *Works*), vol. 7, ed. Franz Hildebrandt (Nashville: Abingdon Press, 1989), 5; Hildebrandt quoted

in Maxine E. Walker, "His Spirit in These Mysterious Leaves: A Wesleyan Way of Reading," in *Proceedings*, Charles Wesley Society (CWS), 5:89. See also the article by Tim Macquiban, "Our God Contracted to a Span: Teaching through Wesleyan Hymns—Incarnated Tools for Spiritual Formation and Theological Education," in *Charles Wesley's Hymns: "Prints" and Practices of Divine Love*, ed. Maxine E. Walker (San Diego: Point Loma Press, 2007), 29–41.

11. Steve Harper, *Devotional Life in the Wesleyan Tradition* (Nashville: Upper Room Books, 1995), 49–50, quoting preface to 1780 *Collection of Hymns* (*Works*, 7:75).

12. Geoffrey Wainwright, *Doxology: The Praise of God in Worship, Doctrine and Life—A Systematic Theology* (New York: Oxford University Press, 1980), 194, 201. See also Frances Young, *Brokenness and Blessing: Towards a Biblical Spirituality* (London: Darton, Longman & Todd, 2007).

13. Charles Wallace, *Susanna Wesley: The Complete Writings* (New York: Oxford University Press, 1997).

14. Charles Wesley hymn, "Give Me the Faith," quoted in Peter Norman Brooks, *Hymns as Homilies* (Leominster: Gracewing, 1997), 71.

15. Daniel W. Hardy and David F. Ford, *Jubilate: Theology in Praise* (London: Darton, Longman & Todd, 1984), 82.

16. Francis Frost, "Biblical Imagery and Religious Experience in the Hymns of the Wesleys," in *Proceedings*, Wesley Historical Society (WHS), 1980:158–66.

17. Henry Bett, *The Hymns of Methodism* (London: Epworth, 1945), 9.

18. Brian Castle, *Sing a New Song to the Lord: The Power and Potential of Hymns* (London: Darton, Longman & Todd, 1994), 11.

19. Thomas Langford quoted by Robert Webster in "Balsamic Virtue: Healing Imagery in Charles Wesley," in Newport and Campbell, *Life, Literature and Legacy*, 231.

20. Macquiban in Walker, *Prints and Practices*, 29–41.

21. Ted A. Campbell, "Charles Wesley, *Theologus*," in Newport and Campbell, *Life, Literature and Legacy*, 264–75.

22. Tyson, "Charles Wesley: An Overview," in Walker, *Prints and Practices*, 92.

23. Gordon W. Lathrop, *Holy Things: A Liturgical Theology* (Minneapolis: Fortress Press, 1989), 99.

24. Paul Ricoeur, *Bible and Imagination in Figuring the Sacred* (Minneapolis: Fortress Press, 1995), quoted in Robinson, *Proceedings*, WHS, 1999–2000: 35–36.

25. J. Richard Watson, *The English Hymn: A Critical and Historical Study* (New York: Oxford University Press, 1999), 226.

26. J. Richard Watson, "The Hymns of Charles Wesley and the Poetic Tradition," in Newport and Campbell, *Life, Literature and Legacy*, 361.

27. Bernard L. Manning, *The Hymns of Wesley and Watts* (London: Epworth, 1942), 29.

28. Theodore W. Jennings, "Transcendence, Justice and Mercy: Toward a (Wesleyan) Reconceptualization of God," in *Rethinking Wesley's Theology for Contemporary Methodism*, ed. Randy L. Maddox (Nashville: Abingdon Press, 1998), 67.

29. M. Douglas Meeks, ed., in his "Introduction: On Reading Wesley with the Poor," *The Portion of the Poor: Good News to the Poor in the Wesleyan Tradition* (Nashville: Abingdon Press, 1995), 17.

30. M. Douglas Meeks, "Sanctification and Economy: A Wesleyan Perspective on Stewardship," in Maddox, *Rethinking Wesley's Theology*, 83–98.
31. Mary Elizabeth Mullino Moore, "Trinity and Covenantal Ministry: A Study of Wesleyan Traditions," in Maddox, *Rethinking Wesley's Theology*, 143–60. See also M. Douglas Meeks, ed., *Trinity, Community, and Power: Mapping Trajectories in Wesleyan Theology* (Nashville: Abingdon Press, 2000).
32. Randy L. Maddox, *Responsible Grace: John Wesley's Practical Theology* (Nashville: Abingdon Press, 1994), 140.
33. M. Douglas Meeks, ed., *Wesleyan Perspectives on the New Creation* (Nashville: Abingdon Press, 2004), 14, 18.
34. Theodore Runyon, *The New Creation: John Wesley's Theology Today* (Nashville: Abingdon Press, 1998), 160–68, 185.
35. Hardy and Ford, *Jubilate*, 165.
36. Wainwright's comment on the 1780 *Collection of Hymns* in *Doxology*, 201.
37. Chilcote, *Wesleyan Tradition*, 10.
38. "Hymns on the Four Gospels and Acts," Hymn 1249, "I Came Not to Call the Righteous," text Luke 5:32, v. 2, in *The Poetical Works of John and Charles Wesley* (hereafter *Poet. Works*), ed. George Osborn, 13 vols. (London: Wesleyan-Methodist Conference, 1858–72), 11:149.
39. Teresa Berger, *Theology in Hymns? A Study of the Relationship between Doxology and Theology According to a Collection of Hymns for the Use of the People Called Methodists (1780)* (Nashville: Abingdon Press, 1995), 147.
40. Quoted in Brooks, *Hymns as Homilies*, 71.
41. "To the Angel of the Church at Philadelphia," v. 17, *Poet. Works*, 2:355.
42. Chilcote, *Wesleyan Tradition*, 12.
43. Quoted in ST Kimbrough, ed., *Orthodox and Wesleyan Spirituality* (New York: St. Vladimir's Seminary Press, 2002), 270.
44. Berger, *Theology in Hymns*, 110.
45. "Hymns on God's Everlasting Love" (1741), no. 1 and others, *Poet. Works*, 3:5.
46. *Poet. Works*, 3:153.
47. "Pleading the Promise of Sanctification," v. 19, *Poet. Works*, 2:319.
48. "The Love Feast," 2:4, *Poet. Works*, 1:352.
49. "Hymns for Times of Trouble and Persecution" (1745), "Hymns to Be Sung in a Tumult," *Poet. Works*, 4:54.
50. Miroslav Volf, *Work in the Spirit* (New York: Oxford University Press, 1991), 7–12.
51. Sarum Theological Lectures, forthcoming publication (London: Darton, Longman & Todd).
52. "Hymn against Idleness," Hymn 55, last verse, *Poet. Works*, 6:425.
53. "Short Hymns on Select Passages of the Holy Scriptures" (hereafter SHSPHS), Hymns 498, 501, *Poet. Works*, 9:330–32.
54. "Hymn before Work," vv. 2–3, *Poet. Works*, 7:149.
55. "Hymns for Some Called to Earn Their Bread," v. 1, *Poet. Works*, 3:289.
56. SHSPHS, text Joshua 6:20 (re: siege of Jericho), *Poet. Works*, 9:122.
57. Psalm 127, v. 1, *Poet. Works*, 8:243.
58. Hymn 2116, v. 2, *Poet. Works*, 12:24.

59. Luke Bretherton, *Hospitality as Holiness* (London: Ashgate, 2006), 73.
60. Daniel L. Migliore, *Faith Seeking Understanding: An Introduction to Christian Theology* (Grand Rapids: Eerdmans, 1991), 182–84.
61. "Give Me the Faith," no. 421, v. 6, *Works*, 7:596.
62. Lloyd, *Struggle for Methodist Identity*, 20.
63. Ibid., 78.
64. Paul L. Chilcote, *Recapturing the Wesleys' Vision: An Introduction to the Faith of John and Charles Wesley* (Downers Grove, Ill.: InterVarsity Press, 2004), 98, 101.
65. Quoted in Lloyd, *Struggle for Methodist Identity*, 140.
66. Quoted in "Charles Wesley and John Fletcher" by Peter Forsaith in Newport and Campbell, *Life, Literature and Legacy*, 115.
67. "Hymns and Poems on Holy Scripture: Acts," hymns on Acts 14:22; 18:23; 20:35, and others, *Poet. Works*, 2:363, 387, 403.
68. "The People's Prayer for the Methodist Preachers" (1786), 2, v. 9, *Poet. Works*, 3:51.
69. "Christ from Whom All Blessings Flow," v. 3, *Poet. Works*, 1:356.
70. "For a Preacher of the Gospel," Hymn 183, v. 9, *Poet. Works*, 1:356.
71. "Hymns on the Trinity," *Poet. Works*, 7:246.
72. "Hymns from the Gospels," no. 52, v. 1, text Matt. 4:21, *Poet. Works*, 10:159.
73. "Hymn on Lk. 12:42," *Poet. Works*, 11:214.
74. "Hymn on Jn. 4:36," *Poet. Works*, 1:362.
75. "Hymn on Lk. 17:7-8," *Poet. Works*, 11:250.
76. Hymns 230–231 on Matt. 9:37-38, "The Labourers Are Few," *Poet. Works*, 10:230.
77. Hymn 196, "After Preaching to the Newcastle Miners"; Hymn 1, v. 10, *Poet. Works*, 5:115.
78. "Hymn for the Kingswood Colliers," no. 184, *Poet. Works*, 5:390–91.
79. "Hymn on Lk. 1:19," *Poet. Works*, 11:104.
80. "Hymns for the Use of Families," no. 42, *Poet. Works*, 7:47.
81. Volf quoted in Bretherton, *Hospitality as Holiness*, 112.
82. Bretherton, *Hospitality as Holiness*, 136–38.
83. Tim Macquiban, "Methodism and the Poor, 1785–1840" (PhD thesis, Birmingham University, 2000).
84. Martin Groves, "Charles Wesley's Spirituality," in Newport and Campbell, *Life, Literature and Legacy*, 457.
85. Kimbrough, *Orthodox and Wesleyan Spirituality*, 265–85.
86. *Hymns and Sacred Poems*, no. 125, "In the Work," v. 1, *Poet. Works*, 5:19–20.
87. SHSPHS, no. 457, on Ruth 4:9-10, *Poet. Works*, 9:148.
88. Hymn 266, on Matt. 10:40, *Poet. Works*, 9:243.
89. Hymn on Acts 28:7, *Poet. Works*, 2:432.
90. L. Gregory Jones and Kevin R. Armstrong, *Resurrecting Excellence: Shaping Faithful Christian Ministry* (Grand Rapids: Eerdmans, 2006), 78.
91. Arthur Sutherland, *I Was a Stranger: A Christian Theology of Hospitality* (Nashville: Abingdon Press, 2006), xvi.
92. *Works*, 7:81, no. 2.
93. Stephen Rhodes, quoted in Duane Elmer, *Cross Cultural Servanthood: Serving the World in Christlike Humility* (Downers Grove, Ill.: InterVarsity Press, 2006), 43.

94. John A. Newton, "Brothers in Arms: The Partnership of John and Charles Wesley," in Newport, *Life, Literature and Legacy*, 61.
95. Lloyd, *Struggle for Methodist Identity*, 42.
96. Quoted in Joanna Cruikshank, "'The suffering members sympathise': Constructing the Sympathetic Self in the Hymns of Charles Wesley," in Newport and Campbell, *Life, Literature and Legacy*, 245.
97. Newton in Newport and Campbell, *Life, Literature and Legacy*, 66.
98. Gareth Lloyd, "The Letters of Charles Wesley," in Newport and Campbell, *Life, Literature and Legacy*, 341.
99. John Lenton, "Charles Wesley and the Preachers," in Newport and Campbell, *Life, Literature and Legacy*, 93.
100. Quoted in Gary Best, *Charles Wesley: A Biography* (London: Epworth, 2007), 336–37.
101. Lloyd, *Struggle for Methodist Identity*, 158.
102. See John Tyson, "'I Preached at the Cross, as Usual': Charles Wesley and Redemption," in Newport and Campbell, *Life, Literature and Legacy*, 216–24.
103. "Being of Beings, Lord of All," v. 6, in ST Kimbrough and Oliver Beckerlegge, eds., *The Unpublished Poetry of Charles Wesley* (Nashville: Abingdon Press, 1998), 1:274.
104. Hymn 125, "In the Work," v. 1, *Poet. Works*, 5:19–20.
105. "To Be Sung at Work," v. 2; "Servant of All, to Toil for Man," v. 3, *Poet. Works*, 1:172.
106. Hymn 240, text Matt. 10:10, v. 2, *Poet. Works*, 10:234.
107. Lloyd, *Struggle for Methodist Identity*, 35.
108. Quoted by Rack in Newport and Campbell, *Life, Literature and Legacy*, 42.
109. Lloyd, *Struggle for Methodist Identity*, 80.
110. Frances Young, "Inner Struggle: Some Parallels Between the Spirituality of John Wesley and the Greek Fathers," in Kimbrough, *Orthodox and Wesleyan Spirituality*, 164–67.
111. Hymn on Mark 14:49 in Kimbrough, *Unpublished Poetry*, 2:64–65.
112. Hymn 2019, text John 12:27, *Poet. Works*, 12:491.
113. Hymn 3204, v. 4, *Poet. Works*, 13:90.
114. Hymn 2465, v. 1, text Acts 5:30, *Poet. Works*, 12:191.
115. Lloyd, *Struggle for Methodist Identity*, 129.
116. Quoted by Lenton in Newport and Campbell, *Life, Literature and Legacy*, 96.
117. Best, *Charles Wesley: A Biography*, 243.
118. See thesis (Bristol University, 1986) by Tim Macquiban.
119. *Hymns and Sacred Poems*, "The Communion of Saints, Pt. 1: Father, Son, and Spirit, Hear," v. 3, *Poet. Works*, 1:356.
120. Hymn 504, v. 10, Part 4 of "The Communion of Saints," *Works*, 7:694.
121. Berger, *Theology in Hymns*, 162, quoting from Ritschl, *The Logic of Theology*.
122. See Chilcote in *Proceedings*, CWS, 9:67–81; and Hymn 196, text Lev. 8:35, "A Charge to Keep I Have," *Poet. Works*, 9:60.
123. Karen Westerfield Tucker, "Charles Wesley and Worship," *Proceedings*, CWS, 9:83–94.
124. Quoted in Volf, *Work in the Spirit*, 139.

125. Hymn, "Another [Thanksgiving]," v. 2, *Poet. Works*, 2:177.

126. Berger, *Theology in Hymns*, 154.

127. Hymn 122, v. 7, p. 16, and Hymn 180, v. 6, *Poet. Works*, 5:95.

128. Hymn 3383, text 2 Peter 1:10, "Make Your Calling and Election Sure," *Poet. Works*, 1:190.

129. Bretherton, *Hospitality as Holiness*, 108–12.

130. Hymn on Isa. 25, v. 17, *Poet. Works*, 3:153.

131. Tim Macquiban, "Imprisonment and Release in the Writings of the Wesleys," in *Studies in Church History* 40, ed. Kate Cooper and Jeremy Gregory (London: Ecclesiastical History Society, 2004).

132. "Hymns for Those That Seek and Those That Have Redemption in the Blood of Jesus Christ," Hymn 3, v. 3, *Poet. Works*, 4:210.

133. Hymn on Isa. 61, 5, v. 5, *Poet. Works*, 4:297.

134. Hymn 51, "The Pilgrim," v. 6, *Poet. Works*, 4:229.

135. Hymn on Psalm 39, v. 12, *Poet. Works*, 8:90.

136. Watson in Newport and Campbell, *Life, Literature and Legacy*, 372.

137. Hymn 16, text Isa. 25, v. 13, *Poet. Works*, 3:153.

138. Hymn on Rev. 3:17, v. 8, *Poet. Works*, 2:90.

139. "Hymn 139, Jesus the Conqueror Reigns," v. 14, *Poet. Works*, 5:39.

140. Kimbrough, *Unpublished Poetry*, 2:364, text Acts 14:22, v. 4.

141. Ibid., 2:33, text Matt. 20:23, v. 3.

142. "Rejoice the Lord Is King," v. 7, *Poet. Works*, 4:148.

143. Hymn 1466, text Luke 17:7, 8, *Poet. Works*, 10:250.

144. Berger, *Theology in Hymns*, 81ff.

145. Hymn 317, *Works*, 7:472.

146. Frances Young, "Wrestling Jacob," *Brokenness and Blessing: Towards a Biblical Spirituality*, chap. 2 (London: Darton, Longman & Todd, 2007), 34–57.

147. "The Good Samaritan," Kimbrough, *Unpublished Poetry*, 2:122–24.

148. Sutherland, *I Was a Stranger*, 81–83.

149. Kimbrough, *Unpublished Poetry*, 124.

150. "For a Believer, in Worldly Business," v. 1, *Poet. Works*, 4:214–15.

151. Hymn 1361, text Luke 10:40, v. 1, *Poet. Works*, 11:197.

152. "Hymns for Our Lord's Resurrection," no. 3, *Poet. Works*, 4:132–33.

153. "Hymn on the Great Supper," v. 24, *Poet. Works*, 4:277.

154. "Where Shall My Wondering Soul Begin?" v. 7, *Poet. Works*, 1:91, C. W.'s conversion hymn.

155. "Hymn: Groaning for Redemption," v. 6, *Poet. Works*, 2:126.

156. John Cobb, *Grace and Responsibility: A Wesleyan Theology for Today* (Nashville: Abingdon Press, 1995), 26–27.

157. Hymn 6, "The Trial of Faith," v. 5, *Poet. Works*, 5:142.

158. Hymn on Titus 2:24, v. 9, *Poet. Works*, 2:304.

159. "Hymn to Mrs. Naylor," *Poet. Works*, 6:270–71.

160. Hymn 931, text Mark 7:36, *Poet. Works*, 11:9.

161. Hymn 3350, text James 2:25, v. 2, *Poet. Works*, 13:169.

162. Groves in Newport and Campbell, *Life, Literature and Legacy*, 446.

163. Groves, "Charles Wesley's Spirituality," in Newport and Campbell, *Life, Literature and Legacy*, 446–64.

164. Chilcote, *Wesleyan Tradition*, 32.

165. Epitaph at City Road Chapel, London.

166. Quoted in Charles Robertson, *Singing the Faith: The Use of Hymns in Liturgy* (London: Canterbury Press, 1990), 140.

167. Watson, *The English Hymn*, 16.

168. Chilcote, *Recapturing the Wesleys' Vision*, 25.

169. Sutherland, *I Was a Stranger*, 29.

170. Volf, *Work in the Spirit*, 29.

171. Jones and Armstrong, *Resurrecting Excellence*, 143–44.

172. Richard John Neuhaus, quoted in Jones and Armstrong, *Resurrecting Excellence*, 101.

173. "The Church of Christ, in Every Age," *Hymns and Psalms: A Methodist and Ecumenical Hymn Book* (London: Methodist Publishing House, 1983), 804.

5. "To Serve the Present Age, Our Calling to Fulfill"

1. See Wolfram Kistner, "The Power of the Church in the South African Context," in *Outside the Camp: A Collection of Writings by Wolfram Kistner*, ed. Hans Brandt (Johannesburg: The South African Council of Churches, 1988), 8.

2. Today's English Version.

3. Herbert McGonigle, "Celebrating Civil Freedom," www.lillenasmusic.com/nphweb/html/h20l/articleDisplay.sp?mediaId=2378577.

4. Charles Villa-Vicencio, "Towards a Liberating Wesleyan Social Ethic for South Africa Today," *Journal of Theology for Southern Africa* 68 (September 1989).

5. The first person I heard use the term *global economic apartheid* was the late Dr. Beyers Naude, past SACC General Secretary, founder of the Christian Institute, and dissident Afrikaner cleric. Speaking on the role of the church in postapartheid South Africa and at a conference at UNISA, which preceded the inception of South Africa's Truth and Reconciliation Commission, Dr. Naude warned of the pending economic challenges facing South Africa and especially the international economic system, which he had no hesitation in labeling "global economic apartheid."

6. Joerg Rieger in Joerg Rieger and John J. Vincent, eds., *Methodist and Radical: Rejuvenating a Tradition* (Nashville: Kingswood Books, 2003), 26.

7. The slave trade ended in the second half of the nineteenth century; the process that led to the abolition began much earlier. A combination of factors led to the demise of the slave trade including liberal opposition in Europe and the Americas that saw the injustices and exploitation of slaves. Tropical supplies, however, grew in demand, and in order to meet the supply of European markets, it was more profitable to leave Africans in Africa to be producers for Europe and the United States. See a similar account, for example, in Toyin Falola, *Key Events in Africa: A Reference Guide* (Westport: Greenwood Press, 2002), 26–27.

8. "Against Global Apartheid: South Africa Meets the World Bank," *IMF and International Finance* (Cape Town: University of Cape Town Press, 2003), 27.

9. Eric Toussaint and Damien Millet, article on the Democratic Republic of Congo, June 23, 2007.

10. Wilf Wilde, *Crossing the River of Fire: Mark's Gospel and Global Capitalism* (London: Epworth, 2006), 119ff.

11. See Rogate Mshana, "Alternatives to Economic Globalization Are Imperative," in A. Bendana et al., *Global Justice: The White Man's Burden?* (Bergen: Fagbokforlaget, 2007), 19–20.

12. Ibid., 55f.

13. Ibid., 56.

14. Dr. Molefe Tsele, former general secretary of the South African Council of Churches, in calling for the formation of a Save Jobs Campaign with the Congress of South African trade unions in 2005, highlighted the plight of South Africa losing 70,000 jobs in two years in the clothing and textile workers' sector while, at the same time, the clothing retail trade, through imports, returned booming profits that ironically included retail sector CEOs earning salaries in excess of US$20 million annually.

15. See, for instance, the useful resource in this regard by John Mihevc, *The Market Tells Them So: The World Bank and Economic Fundamentalism in Africa* (Accra: Third World Network, 1995).

16. See a vivid illustration of the power system of the global neoliberal capitalist economy in Ulrich Duchrow, *Alternatives to Global Capitalism: Drawn from Biblical History, Designed for Political Action* (Heidelberg: Kairos Europa, 1995), 118–19.

17. See also the erudite warning two decades ago by F. J. Hinkelammert, *The Ideological Weapons of Death: A Theological Critique of Capitalism* (Maryknoll, N.Y.: Orbis, 1986).

18. See Ulrich Duchrow, "Political and Economic Wellbeing and Justice: A Global View," in *Studies in Christian Ethics: Political Ethics*, vol. 3, no. 1 (Edinburgh: T&T Clark, 1990), 61–92.

19. Puleng LenkaBula, *Botho/Ubuntu and Justice as Resources for Activism Towards a Just and Sustainable Economy in South Africa and Africa* (Marshalltown, South Africa: Ecumenical Service for Socio-Economic Transformation [ESSET], 2006), 19–20.

20. See the Preface by Desmond Lesejane, director of ESSET, in Puleng LenkaBula, *Botho/Ubuntu and Justice*, 3–4.

21. See Joerg Rieger in Rieger and Vincent, *Methodist and Radical*, 27.

22. See Appendix 3, "The Poor and the People Called Methodists: An Exhibit," in Richard P. Heitzenrater, ed., *The Poor and the People Called Methodists: 1729–1999* (Nashville: Kingswood Books, 2002), 231.

23. See Theodore Jennings, *Good News to the Poor: John Wesley's Evangelical Economics* (Nashville: Abingdon Press, 1990).

24. See Randy L. Maddox, " 'Visit the poor': John Wesley, the Poor, and Sanctification of Believers," in Heitzenrater, ed., *The Poor and the People Called Methodists*, 59–81.

25. See Peter J. Storey, "Why in the World Would You Want to Be a Methodist If You're Not a Wesleyan?" in Purity Malinga and Neville Richardson, eds.,

Rediscovering Wesley for Africa: Themes from John Wesley for Africa Today (Pretoria: Methodist Church of Southern Africa, 2005), 23.

26. John Perkins, *Confessions of an Economic Hit Man* (San Francisco: Berrett-Koehler, 2004).

27. Thomas Jackson, ed., *The Works of the Rev. John Wesley*, M.A., 3rd ed., 14 vols. (Grand Rapids: Baker, 1979).

28. See Outler, ed. *John Wesley* (Oxford: Oxford University Press, 1964), 85-86. The letter in full reads as follows:

> Dear Sir, Unless the divine power has raised you up to be as Athanasius contra mundum, I see not how you can go through your glorious enterprise in opposing that execrable villainy which is the scandal of religion, of England and of human nature. Unless God has raised you up for this very thing, you will be worn out by the opposition of men and devils. But "if God be for you, who can be against you?" Are all of them together stronger than God? O "be not weary in well doing!" Go on, in the name of God and in the power of his might. Till even American slavery (the vilest that ever saw the sun) shall vanish away before it. Reading this morning a tract, wrote by a poor African, I was particularly struck by that circumstance, that a man who has a black skin, being wronged or outraged by a white man, can have no redress, it being a law, in all our colonies, that the oath of a black against a white goes for nothing. What villainy is this? That He who has guided you from your youth up, may continue to strengthen you in this and all things, is the prayer of, Your affectionate servant, John Wesley

29. Rustenberg conference 1987; recorded in JTSA and the Methodist Heritage Day document.

30. See Itumeleng Mosala, "Wesley Read from the Experience of Social and Political Deprivation in South Africa," *Journal for Theology for Southern Africa* 68 (September 1989): 87ff.

31. For a full account relating Mr. Wesley's ability to analyze the political economy of his time and its possible implications for South Africa today, see Keith A. Vermeulen, "Wesleyan Heritage, Public Policy and the Option of Poverty Eradication," in Neville Richardson and Purity Malinga, eds., *Rediscovering Wesley for Africa*, 159–74.

32. LenkaBula, *Botho/Ubuntu and Justice*, 24–25.

33. The full text of Steve de Gruchy's address may be found at www.sacc.org.za/news07/oikos.html.

6. Christian Perfection: A Methodist Perspective on Ecclesiology

1. Albert Outler, "Do Methodists Have a Doctrine of the Church?" in *Doctrine of the Church*, ed. Dow Kirkpatrick (New York: Abingdon Press, 1964).

2. John Wesley, *A Plain Account of Christian Perfection* (hereafter *PACP*) (Kansas City: Beacon Hill, 1966).

3. Percy Livingstone Parker, ed., *The Journal of John Wesley* (Chicago: Moody Press, 1974), 419.

4. "The Adamic law . . . required that man should use, to the glory of God, all the powers with which he was created. Now, he was created free from any defect, either in his understanding or his affections. His body was then no clog to the mind. . . . Consequently, this law, proportioned to his original powers, required that he should always think, always speak, and always act precisely right, in every point whatever. . . . he was well able to do so." Wesley, *PACP*, 79.
5. Ibid. Again and again in *A Plain Account of Christian Perfection* Wesley equates Christian perfection with the renewed image of God, and this image itself with love. See, for example, 28, 32, 51, 55, 60, 81, 91.
6. Ibid., 59.
7. The reference is to Charles Wesley's hymn, "Come, O Thou Traveler Unknown."

7. Human Rights, Vocation, and Human Dignity

1. Ian Brownlie, *Principles of Public International Law*, 6th ed. (New York: Oxford University Press, 2003), 529–33.
2. David Hollenbach, *The Common Good and Christian Ethics* (New York: Cambridge University Press, 2002), 159–64.
3. Michael Perry, *Toward a Theory of Human Rights* (New York: Cambridge University Press, 2007), 33–36.
4. John Nurser, *For All Peoples and Nations: The Ecumenical Church and Human Rights* (Washington, D.C.: Georgetown University Press, 2005), 143–71.
5. Jacques Maritain, *Man and the State* (Chicago: University of Chicago Press, 1951), 76–80.
6. Sam Harris, *The End of Faith* (New York: Norton, 2004).
7. Stanley Hauerwas, *After Christendom? How the Church Is to Behave If Freedom, Justice, and a Christian Nation Are Bad Ideas* (Nashville: Abingdon Press, 1991).
8. See "What If Wesley Was Right?" in this volume.
9. John Howard Yoder, *The Politics of Jesus* (Grand Rapids: Eerdmans, 1971).
10. The definitive analysis of Wesley's understanding of "natural," as opposed to legal or "civil," rights is found in Theodore R. Weber, *Politics in the Order of Salvation: Transforming Wesleyan Political Ethics* (Nashville: Kingswood Books, 2001), 303–52.
11. ST Kimbrough and Oliver A. Beckerlegge, eds., *The Unpublished Poetry of Charles Wesley*, vol. 1 (Nashville: Kingswood Books, 1988), 279. The 2007 Oxford Institute of Methodist Theological Studies heard a performance of "To Dr. Boyce," set to music by Mary Jackson, as part of its celebration of the three hundredth anniversary of Charles Wesley's birth.
12. Wesley, *Works* (Jackson), 11:74–76.
13. Herbert Schlossberg, *The Silent Revolution and the Making of Victorian England* (Columbus: Ohio State University Press, 2000), 28–46.
14. Gertrude Himmelfarb, *The Idea of Poverty: England in the Early Industrial Age* (New York: Knopf, 1984), 31–34.

15. Gertrude Himmelfarb, *The De-Moralization of Society* (New York: Knopf, 1995), 143–44. Donald B. Marti, "Rich Methodists: The Rise and Consequences of Lay Philanthropy in the Mid-Nineteenth Century," in *Perspectives on American Methodism*, ed. Richey, Rowe, and Schmidt (Nashville: Kingswood Books, 1993), 265–85.

16. John Wesley, *Sermons* (Abingdon Press), 1:537. Bishop Hope Morgan Ward made this the theme of her sermon to the Oxford Institute of Methodist Theological Studies on August 19, 2007.

17. See Ivan Abrahams, " 'To Serve the Present Age, Our Calling to Fulfill': A Different Church for a Different World," Chapter 5 in this volume.

18. See Paulo Ayres Mattos, " 'The World Is My Parish'—Is It? Wesleyan Ecclesio-Missiological Considerations from a Contemporary Latin American Perspective," chapter 8 in this volume.

19. Clive Marsh, *Christ in Focus* (London: SCM Press, 2005), 185–86.

20. See Will Willimon, "What If Wesley Was Right?," Chapter 2 of this volume.

8. "The World Is My Parish"—Is It?

1. John Wesley, "Causes of the Inefficacy of Christianity" in *The Works of John Wesley* (hereafter *Works*), ed. Albert C. Outler, 4:87, 90, 93, 95, 96.

2. John Wesley, eds., Frank Baker, Albert Outler, Franz Hildebrandt, Oliver A. Beckerlegge, Gerald R. Cragg, W. Reginald Ward, and Richard P. Heitzenrater (Nashville: Abingdon Press, 1984); *Works*, 25:616.

3. John Wesley, *The Works of John Wesley* [hereafter *Works* (Jackson), ed., Thomas Jackson (Grand Rapids: Baker Books, 1996), 8:310.

4. John Wesley, *Larger Minutes of Several Conversations, Minutes of the Methodist Conferences from the first held in London, by the late Rev. John Wesley, A.M., in the year 1744* (London: John Mason, at the Wesleyan Conference Office, 1862–64), 1:446.

5. Albert C. Outler, "Do Methodists Have a Doctrine of the Church?" in *The Doctrine of the Church*, ed. Dow Kirkpatrick (Nashville: Abingdon Press, 1964), 11–28.

6. David Carter, *Love Bade Me Welcome: A British Methodist Perspective on the Church* (Peterborough, U.K.: Epworth Press, 2002), vii. R. Newton Flew, ed., *The Nature of the Church: Papers Presented to the Theological Commission Appointed by the Continuation Committee of the World Conference on Faith and Order* (London: SCM Press, 1952); Colin Williams, *John Wesley's Theology Today* (New York: Abingdon Press, 1960); Reginald Kissack, *Church or No Church? A Study of the Development of the Concept of Church in British Methodism* (London: Epworth Press, 1964); Frank Baker, *John Wesley and the Church of England* (London: Epworth, 2000); Geoffrey Wainwright. *Methodists in Dialogue* (Nashville: Kingswood Books, 1995); *The Ecumenical Moment: Crisis and Opportunity for the Church* (Grand Rapids: W. B. Eerdmans Pub. Co., 1983); "Methodism's Ecclesial Location and Ecumenical Vocation," in *One in Christ*, vol. 19, no. 2 (1983), 104–34; David Carter, *Love Bade Me Welcome: A British Methodist Perspective on the Church* (Peterborough, England: Epworth Press,

2002); David M. Chapman, *In Search of the Catholic Spirit: Methodists and Roman Catholics in Dialogue* (Peterborough, England: Epworth, 2004).

7. Russell E. Richey, "Understandings of Ecclesiology in United Methodism," paper presented at the twelfth Oxford Institute. Methodist "tradition suffered in the rough and tumble of evangelistic, frontier oriented, camp-meeting dominated Methodism. . . . Experience, conversion, revivalism thus upstaged tradition."

8. A work that in some sense has tried to fill this gap is Russell Richey, Dennis Campbell, and William Lawrence, eds., *United Methodism and American Culture*, 4 vols.; *Connectionalism: Ecclesiology, Mission, and Identity; The People Called Methodist: Forms and Reforms of Their Life; Questions for the Twenty-first-century Church: Doctrines and Discipline; Marks of Methodism: Theology in Ecclesial Practice* (Nashville: Abingdon Press, 1997–2005).

9. Kissack, *Church or No Church?*, 114.

10. Albert Outler, *John Wesley's Sermons: An Introduction* (Nashville: Abingdon Press, 1991), 26.

11. Bryan Stone, "Evangelism as Ecclesial Holiness," paper presented at eleventh Oxford Institute.

12. Ibid., 3.

13. Ibid. Stone provocatively affirms, "The criterion for measuring Christian evangelism is not 'effectiveness' in reaching the world or 'winning' people for Christ. Indeed, as the cross makes abundantly clear, Christians are not called to 'win.'" Therefore, in order to challenge the prevailing evangelistic practices in most of our churches' outreach programs, practices that reflect the logic of "liberal, philosophical, and capitalist economic assumptions about history and about the nature of the self and its agency in the world, . . . the logic of evangelism must be the logic of witness rather than the logic of accomplishment, the only criteria governing such logic being faithfulness and incarnation, rather then sheer effectiveness."

14. Rui Josgrilberg. "A Motivação Originária da Teologia Wesleyana: O Caminho da Salvação," *Caminhando* 8, no. 12 (2 Semestre de 2003): 103-24.

15. Albert Outler, *John Wesley* (New York: Oxford University Press, 1964), 306–7. According to Outler, Wesley's expositions of the doctrine of the church, published in the form of sermons and tracts, have "more to do with the practical issues of churchmanship than with its theological foundations. . . . In all this material the only distinctively Wesleyan accent is the insistence that the church is best defined *in action*, in her witness and mission, rather than by her form of polity." Outler, however, also recognizes that "despite his own irregular position in the Church of England, Wesley seems never to have felt the need to amend the basic ecclesiology which he had developed at Epworth and Oxford, *before* the rise of the Methodist societies."

16. Randy Maddox, "Social Grace: The Eclipse of the Church as a Means of Grace in American Methodism," in *Methodism in Its Cultural Milieu*, ed. Tim Macquiban (Oxford: Applied Theology Press, Westminster College, 1994), 131: "It is now generally agreed that the fruit of this practical venture was a creative synthesis of Anglican and Moravian/Pietist emphases: namely, an ecclesiological

ideal of small intentional gatherings linked integrally to the corporate worship of the larger Church (*ecclesiola in ecclesia*). What is not as often seen is that this ecclesiological synthesis was more than a pragmatic compromise. Wesley's pastoral insistence on the integral relation between intentional small groups and traditional Christian worship was grounded in his most fundamental convictions about human nature, the human problem, and the Way of Salvation."

17. *Works*, 2:156 [emphasis mine].

18. Randy Maddox, "John Wesley: Practical Theologian?" *Wesleyan Theological Journal*, 23:1&2 (Spring and Fall 1988): 122-47; *Responsible Grace: John Wesley's Practical Theology* (Nashville: Kingswood Books, 1994).

19. Maddox, "Practical Theologian?" 135.

20. *Works*, 2:302.

21. Henry H. Knight, III, *The Presence of God in the Christian Life: John Wesley and the Means of Grace* (Metuchen: Scarecrow Press, 1992), 95.

22. Maddox, *Responsible Grace*, 193.

23. Russell Richey, "The Role of History in the Discipline," *Quarterly Review* 9/4 (Winter 1989), 13.

24. *Works* (Jackson), 13:252.

25. See Frank Lambert, *"Peddler in Divinity": George Whitefield and the Transatlantic Revivals, 1737–1770* (Princeton University Press, 1994).

26. Thomas Langford, *Practical Divinity: Theology in the Wesleyan Tradition* (Nashville: Abingdon Press, 1998), 70-88.

27. See Steven W. Manskar, "Good News to the Poor? The United Methodist Church and the Ministry with the Poor," http://www.gbod.org/hpmc/docs/poor_manskar.pdf.

28. *Works* (Jackson), 13:153.

29. For a later sanction of this process in the formation of The Methodist Church in 1939, see Morris L. Davis, *The Methodist Unification: Christianity and the Politics of Race in Jim Crow Era* (New York: New York University Press, 2007).

30. Russell Richey, *Early American Methodism* (Bloomington: Indiana University Press, 1991), xii. On *The Journal and Letters of Francis Asbury*, ed. Elmer T. Clark, J. Manning Potts, and Jacob S. Payton, eds. (Nashville: Abingdon Press, 1958), 1:191.

31. Ibid.

32. Paul O. Evans, "The Ideology of Inequality: Asbury, Methodism, and Slavery," (PhD diss. Rutgers: State University of New Jersey, 1981), 205.

33. *The Doctrines and Discipline of the Methodist Episcopal Church, 1792* (Philadelphia: Parry Hall, 1792), 47.

34. Asbury would state in 1809, "We are defrauded of great numbers by the pains that are taken to keep the blacks from us; their masters are afraid of the influence of our principles. Would not *amelioration* in the condition and treatment of slaves have produced more practical good to the poor Africans, than any attempt at their *emancipation*?" *The Journal and Letters of Francis Asbury*, 2:536. Asbury's changes on American slavery were vividly exposed in the 1804 General Conference episode narrated by James Jenkins in *Experience, Labours, and Sufferings of Rev. James Jenkins of the South Carolina Conference* (printed for

the author, Columbia, S.C., 1842; lithographed and printed by the State Commercial Printing Company, 1958), 142.

35. Matthews, *Slavery and Methodism*, 28–29.

36. *Discipline of The Methodist Episcopal Church*, 9th ed., 59. Quoted in *History of Methodist Missions: To Reform the Nation*, ed. Wade Crawford Barclay (New York: Board of Missions and Church Extension of The Methodist Church, 1949), 2:79.

37. Richey, *Early American Methodism*, xii.

38. J. Gordon Melton, "The Rise of African American Methodism, 1800–1880: An Initial Demographic Exploration," paper presented at the annual meeting of the Historical Society of The United Methodist Church, July 20-22, 2007, in Chevy Chase, Md.

39. Matthews, *Slavery and Methodism*, 13.

40. Maddox, *Responsible Grace*, 140.

41. Rupert Davies, "Methodist Societies: Developments in the Early Societies," *Works*, 9:14. See also the 1810 diagram of the Methodist itinerant system, designed by G. Stebbins and G. King, Broadside, New York: John Totten, 1810–11 [?], Rare Books Division, The New York Public Library, Astor, Lenox and Tilden Foundations. http://www.loc.gov/exhibits/religion/rel02.html.

42. *Works*, 1:533.

43. Ibid., 13:313-14.

44. Ibid., 1:533. See also *Works* (Jackson), 14:321.

45. Richey, *Early American Methodism*, 17.

46. Ibid.

47. For an elaborated discussion on the nature, role, and importance of camp meeting structures in nineteenth-century Methodism see Ellen Eslinger's *Citizens of Zion: The Social Origins of Camp Meeting Revivalism* (Knoxville: University of Tennessee Press, 1999), and Charles Albert Johnson's *The Frontier Camp Meeting: Religion's Harvest Times* (Dallas: Southern Methodist Press, 1985).

48. On the domestication of North American Methodism, and its accommodation to middle-class respectability, see Gregory Schneider, *The Way of the Cross Leads Home: The Domestication of American Methodism* (Bloomington: Indiana University Press, 1993).

49. Maddox, "Social Grace," 135.

50. Ibid., 131.

51. "The Large Minutes of Several Conversations Published during the Life of Mr. Wesley" in *The Minutes of the Methodist Conferences from the First, Held in London, by the Late Rev. John Wesley. A.M., in the year 1744*, vol. 1 (1744–98) (London: John Mason, at the Conference Office, 1862–64), 446-7.

52. *Minutes of Several Conversations between the Rev. Thomas Coke, LL. D., the Rev. Francis Asbury and Others, at a Conference in December 27, 1784* (Philadelphia: Charles Cist, 1785), 4. "to reform the continent *by* spreading the scriptural holiness over these lands," in Barclay, *History of Methodist Missions*, 8 [emphasis mine].

53. Evans, *The Ideology of Inequality*, 223.

54. The North American Methodist emphasis on the continent is explained in more detail in Richey's "Methodism as New Creation: An Historical-Theological Enquiry," in *Wesleyan Perspectives on the New Creation*. ed. M. Douglas Meeks (Nashville: Abingdon Press, 2004), 73–92.

55. Homi K. Babha, *The Location of Culture* (London and New York: Routledge, 1994), 246.

56. *Letters*, A Letter to Francis Asbury, London, 25 November 1787, 8:24. See also *Works*, 2:67.

57. Elmer T. Clark, *An Album of the Methodist History* (New York: Cokesbury Press, 1952), 247.

58. Albert C. Outler, "Methodism in the World Christian Community," in *The Wesleyan Theological Heritage*, ed. Thomas C. Oden and Leicester R. Longden (Grand Rapids: Zondervan, 1991), 249.

59. See Walter Wink, *Naming the Powers, Unmasking the Powers, Engaging the Powers*, 3 vols. (Philadelphia: Fortress, 1984–92).

LIST OF AUTHORS

Ivan Abrahams is the Presiding Bishop of the Methodist Church of Southern Africa and chair of the South African Church Leaders Forum. He has engaged questions of globalization and culture in various research centers.

Lung-kwong Lo is the Director of the Divinity School of Chung Chi College, the Chinese University of Hong Kong and the President of The Methodist Church, Hong Kong. His recent publications include "Heaviness through Manifold Temptations" in *Forty-four Sermons to Serve the Present Age* (Epworth); "Paul's Gospel to the Gentiles and Its Implications for Christian Mission to Chinese" in *Text and Task: Scripture and Mission* (Paternoster); "The Nature of the Issue of Ancestral Worship among Chinese Christians" in *Studies in World Christianity* (Edinburgh University Press).

Robin W. Lovin is Cary Maguire University Professor of Ethics at Southern Methodist University and former Dean of SMU's Perkins School of Theology. He is the author of *Reinhold Niebuhr and Christian Realism* (Cambridge), *Christian Ethics: An Essential Guide* (Abingdon), and *Christian Realism and the New Realities* (Cambridge).

Tim Macquiban presently serves as Minister at Wesley Methodist Church, Cambridge, UK, and Chaplain to University students and Wesley House. He was previously Principal of Sarum College, Salisbury, UK. He has published contributions in *Methodism and Education: From Roots to Fulfillme*nt (Kingswood, 2000) and *The Poor and the People Called Methodists* (Kingswood, 2002). He is a Co-Chair of the Oxford Institute of Methodist Theological Studies.

Paulo Ayres Mattos is a Bishop (Emeritus) of the Methodist Church in Brazil. He is a professor of Systematic Theology on the Faculty of Theology of the Methodist Church, Methodist University of São Paulo, Brazil.

M. Douglas Meeks is the Cal Turner Chancellor Professor of Theology and Wesleyan Studies, Vanderbilt University Divinity School, Nashville, Tennnessee. His publications include *Origins of the Theology of Hope* (Fortress), *God the Economist: The Doctrine of God and Political Economy* (Fortress), and editor, *Trinity, Community, and Power: Mapping Trajectories of Wesleyan Theology* (Kingswood), and *Wesleyan Perspectives on the New Creation* (Kingswood).

Marjorie Hewitt Suchocki is Professor emerita, Claremont School of Theology, Claremont, California. She directs the Process and Faith Center and the Whitehead International Film Festival, both programs of the Center for Process Studies at Claremont School of Theology. Her most recent books are *Sin and Cinema: Exploring the Human Condition in Film and Theology* (Abingdon), *A Perfect Love: Understanding John Wesley's Plain Account of Christian Perfection*, with Steven Manskar and Diane Hinson (United Methodist Publishing House), and *Divinity and Diversity: A Christian Affirmation of Religious Pluralism* (Abingdon).

William H. Willimon is Presiding Bishop of the North Alabama Conference of The United Methodist Church, Birmingham, Alabama Area and Visiting Research Professor at Duke Divinity School, Durham, North Carolina. Prior to his current position he served for twenty years as Professor of Christian Ministry and Dean of Duke University Chapel. He is a General Editor of the *Wesley Study Bible* (Abingdon) and author of fifty books. His articles have appeared in many publications including *The Christian Ministry, Quarterly Review, Liturgy, Worship*, and *Christianity Today*. His Pulpit Resource is used each week by over eight thousand pastors in the U.S., Canada, and Australia. In a recent Baylor University survey, he was named one of the "Twelve Most Effective Preachers in the English-Speaking World."

LaVergne, TN USA
13 September 2009
157648LV00003B/22/P